D0708281

WITHDRAWN

TEACHING
FASTER READING

TEACHING
FASTER READING

A MANUAL

BY

EDWARD FRY, PH.D.

Director, Reading Clinic
Loyola University of Los Angeles
Fulbright Lecturer, Makerere University College
Kampala, Uganda

CAMBRIDGE
AT THE UNIVERSITY PRESS
1963

PUBLISHED BY
THE SYNDICS OF THE CAMBRIDGE UNIVERSITY PRESS

Bentley House, 200 Euston Road, London, N.W. 1
American Branch: 32 East 57th Street, New York 22, N.Y.
West African Office: P.O. Box 33, Ibadan, Nigeria

Printed in Great Britain at the University Press, Cambridge
(Brooke Crutchley, University Printer)

CONTENTS

INTRODUCTION

This book is intended to help teachers give a course in reading improvement at either the secondary-school or university level. It may also be used as a text by teachers in training who can improve their own reading skills at the same time as they learn how to improve those of their future students. Finally the book may be used as a do-it-yourself reading improvement programme by any adult or older student. Previous training in teaching reading is not assumed.

Teaching Faster Reading is written to accompany the students' book *Reading Faster—A Drill Book* (Cambridge University Press, 1963) but the methods, course outline, and lecture material will work with a number of other students' drill books.

This book concentrates on the improvement of reading speed while making certain that the fundamental requirement of normal comprehension is not neglected. It is intended to supplement and not supplant other methods of teaching the understanding of written English, such as language study and literary criticism.

One of the major methods of improving both speed and comprehension is to set the students to work through a series of timed reading passages followed by comprehension questions. These passages are provided in the *Drill Book*. But in addition to the timed reading and comprehension drill, the student needs both encouragement and information about reading. The teacher will have to use his art and skill as an educator to provide the encouragement, and some learning discipline; while this teachers' book will provide material both for the teacher's own information and for classroom lectures.

The book is divided into ten chapters, as reading-improvement courses often cover a ten-week period. If the teacher sets three lessons a week out of the *Drill Book*, as is suggested, this too will cover a period of ten weeks. But the teacher may choose either to extend the course or to compress it to a somewhat shorter period, according to the problems of the individual school. Reading-improvement courses are seldom shorter than six or seven weeks and seldom longer than eighteen weeks, with most courses lasting about ten weeks. If a course is too short there is hardly time for enough practice and ingraining of the desired skills and habits. If the course is stretched out too long the student loses interest and becomes bored with the whole topic. Spreading the course over too long a period keeps it from picking up the critical momentum that can be seen in the week-by-week improvement in the class average.

The amount of class-time that the teacher devotes to the reading-improvement course will vary from school to school. It is suggested that the teacher take not less than two half-hour periods per week. There will also be a modest amount of homework required in addition to these class sessions. Usually one of the weekly class sessions will be a lecture and discussion based on the chapters of this book. The other class session will be a timed reading exercise done in class from the *Drill Book*, together with a check and discussion of the homework. The teacher may also wish to place some emphasis on comprehension by getting the class to discuss the answers to the test questions after the class has completed the exercise.

In addition to timed reading exercises and lectures, many reading-improvement courses also use tachistoscopic drill. This consists of flashing words, phrases and sometimes symbols on a screen for about one-twentyfifth of a second using a special device known as a tachistoscope. A simple but usable tachistoscope consists of an ordinary slide-projector, a shutter fitted in front of the lens and acting like a camera shutter, and a specially prepared set of filmstrips. Though not all reading authorities agree on the necessity of using a tachistoscope, many reading instructors find tachistoscopic drill helpful in maintaining interest in the reading-improvement course and in breaking up slow word-by-word reading habits. In conducting reading-improvement courses I myself usually use tachistoscopic drill, consisting mainly of words and phrases of increasing length, for about 25 minutes each week. (See manuals and materials prepared by 'Learning Through Seeing', Box 368, Sunland, California, U.S.A.)

There are some successful courses aimed at improving reading speed and comprehension which do not use any mechanical aids such as the tachistoscope; but none of them is conducted without timed reading exercises and some lectures.

ANSWERS TO QUESTIONS FREQUENTLY ASKED BY STUDENTS AND TEACHERS

How much gain in speed can I expect from taking this course?

The author's courses in the United States and Africa usually increase speed by an average of 100%; that is, the class average roughly doubles. This is normal for such work in the United States and Britain. For example, C. Poulton, writing in the *British Journal of Educational Psychology* in 1961, after surveying the results of 40 classes in eight different settings, including industrial concerns, technical colleges, nursing colleges and university extra-mural departments (ranging from 15 to 27 hours of instruction), writes: 'Looking at the data from all institutions, the average reading normally started at between 160 and 280 words per minute, and ended at between 340 and 500 words per minute, giving increases of between 40 and 130 per cent.'

Does reading faster lower comprehension?

Generally not. Most of the author's classes begin and end at nearly the same normal level of comprehension. The African classes showed some gain in comprehension, but their comprehension was at first a little on the low side. For British students Poulton says: 'There was more often a gain than a loss in comprehension as measured by the multiple-choice questions.'

Does training on one type of reading matter, such as easy factual material, help to improve reading on other types of material?

The author once conducted a course for employees of a research organization, and both before the course and after the course a company psychologist tested the students on very difficult reading material (on the theory of games). The author found that the students made a gain of about 100% on relatively easy factual material, while the psychologist found that their gain on very difficult material was about 90%, even though no training was given on difficult reading material. The actual rate in words per minute was of course slower on the difficult material than on the easier material. Further proof of the general help given by reading-improvement courses is that over 80% of United States institutions of higher learning offer some such course, and the courses are rapidly spreading in secondary schools. A more concrete example is the letter received from a former student which said that it was being written in 'saved time', for he could now go through his morning mail and business reports in half the time he needed before taking the reading-improvement course.

Will reading-improvement training in one language help the students to improve their reading in another language?

Michael West in his book *Learning to Read a Foreign Language* (Longmans) found that training Indian students to improve their reading in English also substantially improved their reading in Bengali. He concluded that 'Reading ability is a general power. It is not confined to one language, for improvement in the ability to read one language is "transferred" and shows itself in improvement of the reading of another language.' The answers to this and the preceding question show that it is not necessary to train on a single precise type of reading material for reading skill to be widely transferred.

Can you be too old to learn to improve your reading?

The author has taught essentially the same course to groups varying from United States high school seniors (16- to 18-year-olds) to senior management executives in industry. In adult education work there is frequently a 16-year-old sitting next to a 60-year-old and there is no perceptible difference in their improvement scores. This is amplified by Poulton, who reports that 'A group of 26 students from the Scottish College of Commerce showed no difference between over- and under-40's'.

Do individual differences effect reading improvement?

Yes; as might be expected, the more intelligent and enthusiastic students do better. Though this course will help duller or backward students, it is more specifically designed for normal and above average students (as part of a total language-improvement programme).

Shall I be able to keep the reading improvement I make?

Studies in the United States, where students were tested for reading speed and comprehension after six months or one year, generally showed between 60 and 100% retention of the gain, according to the group, type of course, and type of test used. Studies in Britain show essentially the same results.

Poulton reports that one investigator found a 93% retention of gain after 13 weeks, while another found a 61% retention of gain after six or more months (using essay questions). He concludes, 'A moderate reduction in the average speed of reading without much change in comprehension will probably be found to be the rule. This would still be a reasonably satisfactory outcome.'

SUMMARY OF INTRODUCTION

1. This book is for classes at the secondary-school and university level.

2. The main method of reading improvement is by using timed reading passages followed by comprehension tests.

3. The teacher must provide:
   (*a*) Encouragement and discipline.
   (*b*) Information on reading provided in this manual.

4. Courses usually last ten weeks.

5. This manual has ten chapters.

6. Two weekly class sessions might include one lecture and one timed exercise.

7. Homework of two exercises per week, and sometimes additional homework, is set.

8. Additional class-time may be used to teach comprehension by discussing test questions.

9. Tachistoscopic drill may be used.

10. Students may hope to double their reading speed.

11. Reading faster does not usually lower comprehension.

12. Training in one type of reading matter, and one language, helps to improve reading of other types and other languages.

13. Students may learn to improve their reading at any age, and whatever their present standard in reading.

14. A high proportion of the improvement made is likely to be retained.

1

THE IMPORTANCE OF
READING FASTER

One of the most important functions of the teacher is to provide 'sales talk' for reading improvement. 'You can lead a horse to water but you cannot make him drink.' Students are often at school because the law requires it or because they are working for a certificate or diploma. They must be made to realize the importance of reading improvement.

If the students do not co-operate with the course, try to improve, and do their homework diligently, their reading will not improve. So the teacher must get them on his side and working to improve themselves. This should be fairly easy: one can point out to them that much of their homework consists of reading; that if they go further in their education much reading will be required of them; and that as adults they will probably do much reading, both for business and pleasure, of newspapers, magazines, books and directions. One can suggest the extent to which modern society depends on the ability to communicate through reading: every government official, business man and housewife must read and does read. One might give some examples from the students' own community.

Writing is used as a means of communication, because with it one man can share his knowledge with millions. Furthermore, it is fairly cheap, since modern printing-presses can make all types of material available at a fairly low cost. From the reader's standpoint, reading should be one of the fastest methods of receiving information. English is usually spoken at about 150 words per minute, while an average person in England or the United States can read at 250 words per minute or faster. So we see that an average person can read nearly twice as fast as he can listen. Speakers of English as a second language can easily learn to read at that speed, or even faster.

	1st week		7th week		Gain	
	Speed (w.p.m.)	Comprehension (%)	Speed (w.p.m.)	Comprehension (%)	Speed (w.p.m.)	Comprehension (%)
B.A. Science	171	56	385	77	214	21
B.A. Arts	220	65	370	72	150	7
Mixed B.A. and sixth form	201	63	395	75	194	12
Sixth form	154	40	381	70	227	10

Table 1. Reading-speed and comprehension improvement of four classes at Makerere University College after 7 weeks of instruction. (Classes were approximately 85 % African students and 15 % Asian. Sixth-form classes are students about 18 years old in a senior secondary school who are preparing for the university in one or two years.)

These reading-improvement scores are based on exercises found in the *Drill Book* and given under classroom conditions. There is some evidence that students, when relaxing at home, do not read as rapidly as they do in class under test conditions but there is also evidence that a good deal of the reading improvement shown in class tests transfers to other types of reading, such as that done for recreation or study.

Even if these improvement figures seem ambitiously high, the teacher might suggest that students could at any rate improve their reading by 25 %. This would mean that in the time normally taken to read four books they could now read five. In the course of a lifetime this could mean important time-saving or increased reading. Doing a few arithmetic problems on the board with the students' own estimate of the amount of time they spend reading per week will be quite convincing.

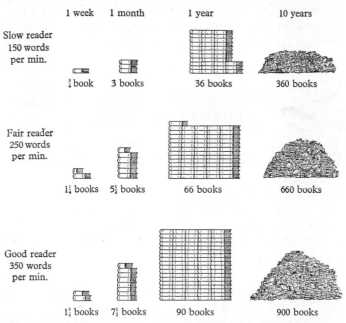

Fig. 1. Sample arithmetic problems showing benefits of increased speed. (These problems assume that the student reads 1 hour per day, 6 days per week; and that the books read are of an average length of 70,000 words.)

Some students may feel that fast readers do not understand as much as slow readers. This fallacy can easily be disproved when you give the first reading test in class. A quick glance at the scores will show that fast readers sometimes have very good comprehension and sometimes poor comprehension. Some slow readers will have good comprehension and others poor comprehension. In short, there is little relationship between

3

reading speed and comprehension. This statement needs to be made with caution because sometimes when a slow reader suddenly improves his reading speed it will *temporarily* lower his comprehension (this will be discussed in later chapters). But the essential point for the class to grasp is that fast readers can certainly comprehend as much as, or more than, slow readers.

SUMMARY AND SUGGESTED LECTURE OUTLINE

WEEK I, SESSION I

1. The importance of reading in school, for pleasure, or for business.
2. Give local examples.
3. Reading is the fastest form of communication—twice as fast as listening.
4. Reading courses can often double speed without losing comprehension.
5. The teacher may work arithmetic problems on the board using students' estimate of the time spent reading per week, year, etc., using speed increases of 25, 50, 100%.
6. The teacher may also wish to discuss the course with the class (see Introduction summary, p. xii).

INITIAL READING TEST

For the good of the student, the teacher and the administration it is as well to begin the course with as accurate a reading test as possible. Since the object of the course is to show some improvement in reading speed and sometimes in comprehension as well, it is necessary to have some measure of the students' reading speed and comprehension at the beginning of the course. This can be obtained by using the first exercise in the *Drill Book* or a standardized reading test which measures reading speed and comprehension from any other source. If some test other than the first drill passage is used care must be taken in selecting it so that it will be at the correct level of difficulty.

Fig. 2. Method of showing students their reading time.

If the first drill passage is being used as the first reading test, explain to the students that this is to be a test of both reading speed and comprehension. They are to read the passage as rapidly as possible, and to note down the time taken either in the *Drill Book* itself or on a separate sheet of paper.

Timing of the reading test requires a little careful attention from the teacher, but is not difficult. The first requirement is a watch which has a second hand. On the blackboard the teacher then writes the word 'minutes' and the word 'seconds'. Underneath the word 'seconds' he should write a column of numbers: 0, 10, 20, 30, 40, 50. The teacher then starts the class all at once, saying 'ready—go'. At the same time he glances at his watch and after one minute has passed he writes '1' on the board underneath the word 'minutes'. He then immediately places his finger alongside the zero under the seconds column. Keeping his eye on the watch, he moves his finger down to 10 when 10 more seconds have passed, to 20 when 20 seconds have passed, and so on. When two minutes have passed he quickly erases the '1' under the minute column and writes '2', then continues the same procedure, pointing his finger to the correct number of seconds.

As each student finishes reading his passage he glances up at the board, notes the time that the teacher is indicating, and writes it down in the *Drill Book* or on a separate sheet of paper. It is important that each student should record this time accurately, as it is used to determine his reading speed in words per minute. The teacher should explain carefully how the student is to begin reading when the teacher says 'go' and to look up as soon as he is finished and record the time accurately.

Students should then turn the page and answer the ten multiple-choice questions without looking back at the passage. They should write 'a', 'b', 'c' or 'd', according to their choice of answer either in the *Drill Book* or on a separate sheet of paper. The comprehension questions are not timed, but if one or two of the class continue working long after most have finished a halt should be called, so as not to waste too much time. Extreme slowness is often a measure of poor comprehension and should be penalized a little anyway.

The teacher should not give out the *Drill Book* to the students until he is ready to give the reading test. This will keep the class from looking through the book and becoming familiar with the test material. After the books have been given out the teacher should tell the students not to read on beyond the passage which is set. The teacher should decide whether the books are to be written in or not. It is easier and neater to let the readers do all the work in the *Drill Book*, but sometimes for the sake of economy and re-use of the *Drill Book* the teacher may tell the students to do all writing on a separate sheet of paper or in a separate notebook.

The comprehension test is often scored by letting the students exchange papers or books and correct each other's work while the teacher slowly reads out the correct answers. But on a first reading test it is perhaps better for the teacher to correct the comprehension test himself so that there will be less chance of error. A normal comprehension score is 70% (7 out of 10 correct). More discussion of normal comprehension will be given in a later chapter.

A reading score in words per minute can be obtained from entering the table at the end of the *Drill Book*. This table gives the reading rate in words per minute, for every ten- or fifteen-second interval, for articles of various lengths. Each timed passage in the *Drill Book* has the approximate number of words in it at the bottom of the page on which it is printed. The first article, for example, contains 525 words; if a student reads that passage in 3 minutes 15 seconds his reading speed would be 162 words per minute. The paragraph below the table also gives directions for determining the words per minute in other ways, though usually use of the table is the easiest.

The teacher should make a chart listing all the students names down the left-hand side. In the first column after the names, the teacher should put the results of the initial test. The reading speed in words per minute should be placed first followed by an oblique stroke and the reading comprehension score as a percentage. Each week, as the students take their test in class, the teacher adds each student's speed and comprehension score to the chart. This chart is an easy way to follow each student's progress as well as a record for the class as a

7

Time	Length of article in words								
(min. sec.)	425	450	**475**	500	525	550	575	600	625
0 50	511	540	569	600	638	657	686	720	748
1 00	425	450	475	500	525	550	575	600	625
1 10	365	387	407	427	450	471	493	515	535
1 20	319	338	356	375	394	412	433	450	469
1 30	284	300	316	334	350	364	384	400	415
1 40	256	271	285	300	316	330	345	360	376
1 50	232	246	260	273	287	300	314	328	342
2 00	213	225	247	250	262	274	288	300	312
2 10	196	208	**218**	231	242	253	265	276	288
2 20	186	194	204	215	226	236	246	258	268
2 30	170	180	190	200	210	220	230	240	250
2 40	159	169	178	188	198	206	216	225	235
2 50	151	159	166	174	183	192	200	209	218
3 00	142	150	158	167	175	184	192	200	208
3 10	134	142	151	158	166	174	182	190	198
3 20	128	135	143	150	158	165	173	180	188
3 30	122	128	136	143	150	157	165	171	179
3 40	116	123	130	137	143	150	157	164	171
3 50	111	117	124	131	137	144	150	157	163
4 00	106	112	118	125	131	137	144	150	156
4 10	102	108	114	120	126	132	138	144	150
4 20	98	104	110	116	122	127	133	139	145
4 30	94	100	105	111	117	122	128	132	139
4 40	91	97	102	107	113	118	123	128	134
4 50	88	93	98	104	109	114	119	124	129
5 00	85	90	95	100	105	110	115	120	125
5 10	82	87	92	97	102	106	111	116	121
5 20	80	84	89	94	99	104	108	113	117
5 30	77	82	86	91	95	100	105	109	114
5 40	75	79	84	87	93	97	102	106	110
5 50	73	77	82	86	90	94	98	103	107
6 00	71	75	79	83	87	92	96	100	104
6 10	69	73	77	81	85	89	93	97	101
6 20	67	71	75	79	83	87	91	95	99
6 30	65	69	73	77	81	84	88	92	96
6 40	63	68	71	75	79	83	86	90	93
6 50	62	66	70	73	77	81	84	88	91

Fig. 3. 'Words per minute' chart. (If a student reads a 475-word article in 2 minutes 10 seconds his rate is 218 words per minute.)

whole. Each week the teacher should average the reading speed and comprehension scores so that he has an idea how the class is moving.

Name	1st week test	2nd week test	3rd week test	4th week test	5th week test	6th week test	7th week test
Jones	145/60	175/50	185/70	220/80	250/60	275/70	301/60
Smith	262/90	320/80	380/70	385/80	350/60	425/70	495/70
Mboya	177/80	189/80	225/90	185/90	271/60	302/70	350/90
Class average	174/65	189/68	212/67	249/69	293/68	325/70	360/72

Fig. 4. Sample progress chart to be kept by the reader.

HOMEWORK

Finally homework should be set. If the teacher is following the ten-week-course plan, two exercises will be set each week for homework. The students should be told to pay attention to both reading speed and comprehension while doing the homework. They should also be asked to do it at a favourable time, not when they are too tired or the environment too disturbing. The students should be shown how to correct their own comprehension tests by using the key (answers) at the back of the *Drill Book*, and finally each student should keep a record of the speed and comprehension score for each exercise either in the *Drill Book* or in a separate notebook.

One small problem that may arise in giving a reading test or exercise is that some students start to read the test passage before the teacher says 'go'. This can be eliminated by telling all the students to 'look up' at the teacher as soon as they have found the proper page and are ready. The teacher explains that the test cannot begin until all students show that they are ready to begin by 'looking up' at the teacher.

If the question of cheating comes up, tell the student that

the cheater only cheats himself. If he does not wish to do the work honestly and improve his reading; that is his business. The teacher should encourage the students but marks or punishments should not be given. The gain the student makes in improving his reading should be its own reward. A student who does not make a satisfactory gain in reading or comprehension should not be punished, as he may be working near the limits of his ability. But most students are not usually working to their limits.

In doing homework exercises the student will need a watch with a second-hand. The student can write down the starting time in minutes and seconds (often it is easier to start when the second-hand is at 0). Then he can write down his finishing time in minutes and seconds. The difference between the two will be his reading time. He then uses the chart at the back of the *Drill Book* to determine his words per minute score. Usually entering in the chart the time to the nearest ten seconds is accurate enough for drill purposes.

SUMMARY AND SUGGESTED
COURSE WORK

WEEK I, SESSION 2

Directions for reading test

1. Explain that it is a test of reading speed and comprehension. The class should read as rapidly as is consistent with comprehension, for they must answer the questions without looking back.

2. Explain the method of timing. Demonstrate.

3. Tell the students exactly where to record time and answers to comprehension questions (either in the *Drill Book* or on separate paper).

4. The comprehension questions are not timed, but a total time limit may be imposed on a few stragglers.

5. Correct the reading test and record the answers on class progress sheet.

Homework

1. If the teacher is following a ten-week course and using the *Faster Reading Drill Book*, he should set two passages to be done for the week's homework.

2. This homework should be done at a favourable time and scored by the student.

2

COMMON FAULTS AND
EYE MOVEMENTS

There are a number of bad habits which poor readers adopt. Most of these involve using extra body movement in the reading process. In efficient reading, the muscles of the eye should make the only external movement. Of course there must be vigorous mental activity, but extra body movements, such as pointing with the finger or moving the lips, do not help reading and often slow it down.

POINTING AT WORDS

A fault that is often seen when students are trying to concentrate is pointing to the words with a finger, pencil or ruler. Young children and very poor readers often point with a finger at each word in turn. Slightly more mature readers sometimes hold a pencil or ruler underneath the line which they are reading. While marking the line might be helpful for beginning readers, it is certainly unnecessary for normal readers. Besides slowing down the student through the mere mechanical movement of pencil, ruler, or finger, pointing at lines or words tends to cause the student to focus his attention on the wrong thing. The important thing to concentrate on while reading is the idea that the author is trying to communicate, and not the location of the words on the page. The eyes of any child old enough to learn how to read are certainly skilful enough to be able to follow a line of print without extra help from fingers or rulers.

Another common fault that the teacher will be able readily to observe is head movement. This most often occurs when students are nervous about their reading or trying hard, as during a reading speed test. With head movement the student tries to aim his nose at the word he is reading so that as he reads across the line his head turns slightly. When he makes the return sweep to begin a new line his head quickly turns back so that his nose is pointed at the left-hand margin, and he can now begin to read the new line by slowly turning his head. The belief that this head movement aids reading is pure nonsense. Eye muscles are quite capable of shifting the eyes from word to word, and they need no help from neck muscles. I sometimes tease my students by asking them if they have 'radar' in their noses, or if neck muscles are involved in reading comprehension.

Often students are quite unaware that they are moving their heads while reading. The teacher should observe his students while reading drill is in progress, and if he sees a student moving his head while reading he should immediately remind him not to do it.

VOCALIZATION

Vocalization is another fault. Some poor readers think it necessary to pronounce aloud each word as it is read. Usually this pronunciation is quite soft, so that the student is more whispering to himself than actually reading aloud, but even this is very undesirable. The chief disadvantage of pronouncing words while you read them is that it tends to tie reading speed to speaking speed, and as I have already said, the silent reading of most normal readers is nearly twice as fast as their speaking. Usually this fault can be eliminated in older students by their own conscious effort, possibly with the aid of a few reminders from the teacher. Vocalization by beginning readers is a common fault; after a reader reaches some maturity it becomes very undesirable.

Vocalization takes various modified forms. Sometimes a reader will merely move his lips soundlessly. At other times he may make tongue or throat movements without lip movement. Still other readers will have activity going on in their vocal cords, which can be detected by the student if he places his fingers alongside his larynx (vocal cords in the throat) while he is reading. Vocal cord vibration can be felt with the fingers quite easily. You might demonstrate this to your students by getting them to hold their throats while they hum softly. Like true vocalization, these minor parts of 'subvocalization'—lip movement, tongue or throat movement and vocal cord movement—can be stopped by conscious effort on the part of the student. The teacher can often observe lip movement and should remind the student not to do it. Excessively slow reading speeds are often a clue to some type of vocalization.

SUBVOCALIZATION

Finally we come to the most difficult of all types of vocalization. This is subvocalization. In subvocalization there is no body movement. The lips, tongue or vocal cords do not move. But an inner type of speech persists: within the student's mind he is saying each word to himself, clearly pronouncing each word and then listening to himself, as it were. This fault is difficult, but not impossible, to cure.

Probably the main reason for subvocalization is the nature of written language. English is written in an alphabet: a set of symbols which stand for speech-sounds. The speech-sounds in turn stand for an idea or thought. Since most students learn to read either after learning to speak or at the same time, there is a natural tendency to relate the printed word to its speech-sound. But it is not necessary to say or hear the word in order to get its meaning. It is quite possible to look at the printed word and get the idea directly. This is what efficient readers do.

The fault of subvocalization is often contributed to by teachers who equate all reading lessons with reading aloud. It is true that an important part of reading instruction lies in asking the students to read aloud. But this must not be the only type of reading instruction. In fact students should be given much practice in reading silently, because unless they are to be radio announcers, or follow some similar profession, most of the reading they will do in their lives will be silent reading. Some teachers make the situation worse by correcting the student's oral reading so that he is not allowed to leave out a single syllable. The student may read a sentence and obviously gets the sense of it, but the teacher will make him go back and re-read it because he left out one 'the'. Accurate oral reading is a desirable dramatic skill, but it has little relationship to silent reading. Many adults with good education can read novels and text-books and understand them well, yet if asked to read aloud would make a poor showing. An important part of this reading-improvement course should be to divorce oral reading skills from silent reading skills. In this course we are interested in making the student able to grasp quickly the ideas presented on a printed page, and not in making him able to entertain the class or please the teacher by reading aloud without error.

Curing subvocalization

The curing of subvocalization often takes a subtle and roundabout route. First, explain to the class that the real purpose of reading is to understand what the author is saying. Then tell them it is quite possible to do this without pronouncing each word. In fact it is undesirable to pronounce each word because of the time it wastes. It is quite easy to show that many people can read much faster than they could possibly speak; and if this is the second time you have conducted this course in your school you will be able to cite a number of students who can do this. So the first thing that the student needs to realize is that subvocalization is bad.

A direct attack on subvocalization is not always successful. Sometimes when students first become aware of the fact that they are subvocalizing (and this is true in most cases of people reading at speeds of less than 250 words a minute) they try to stop subvocalizing by sheer will-power. They simply say to themselves 'I will not subvocalize'. Often when the student does this he will stop understanding, whereas before, when he was subvocalizing and saying each word inwardly to himself, he was at least taking in the story. Now when he tries by will-power to shut off all subvocalization he may not understand a thing. His eyes may go across the print while nothing happens. As one student expressed it to me, 'the silence was killing me'. If this happens the student should be told to concentrate on the other aspects of reading, namely speed and comprehension. If he must talk to himself while reading let him say, 'What does this mean?', 'I don't believe this', 'This point is not related to the paragraph', or 'I'll bet this will be a question on the comprehension test'. In short, he should talk *about* the material but not repeat the words. He should be mentally engaging in a conversation with the author, but not merely parroting what the author says. Efficient reading requires an active mind, not the mere passivity of saying the author's words.

At the same time that the reader is urgently trying to understand what the author is saying, and testing out the author's ideas against his own background of knowledge, he should be trying to speed up the reading process. He should keep in the back of his mind that one of the purposes of this drill is to get him to read faster, and he should attempt in each exercise to read a little faster than he did in the preceding one. If he is actively and forcefully trying to comprehend the subject-matter, and at the same time to increase his speed, he will have little time left for subvocalization. So there is a positive cure for subvocalization. The negative approach of 'I will not subvocalize' should be replaced by the more positive attitudes of 'I must understand what the author is saying' and 'I must go faster'.

When the eyes are reading a line of print they make a series of short jerky movements along the line, stopping after every one or two words for a very brief pause. The eyes do not, as some

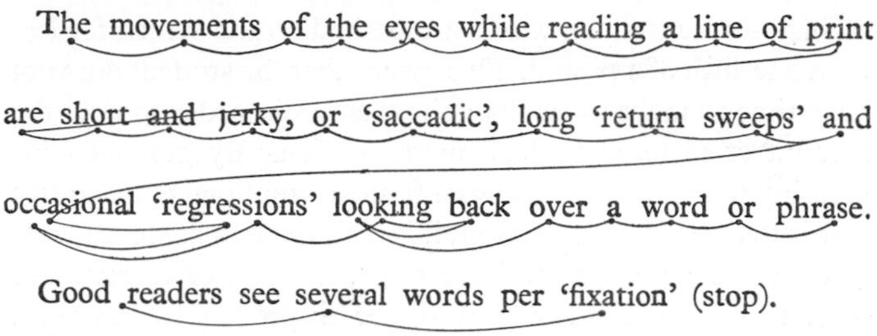

The movements of the eyes while reading a line of print are short and jerky, or 'saccadic', long 'return sweeps' and occasional 'regressions' looking back over a word or phrase.

Good readers see several words per 'fixation' (stop).

Fig. 5. Eye movements while reading. (Good readers make very few regressions.)

people erroneously believe, make a smooth even movement along the line. Each time the eye stops it sees a certain span of material and this span is called the 'span of recognition'. The span of recognition for most readers is a little over one word. If the total number of words in a paragraph is divided by the total number of eye-stops, the ratio will be about 1·25, so we can say that the average person sees about $1\frac{1}{4}$ words per eye-stop or 'fixation', as eye-stops are sometimes called. In actual reading practice this might mean that the student might make one fixation on a word of average size, two fixations on a very long word, and at other times see two short words in one fixation.

Since the length of a fixation is fairly constant for all human beings, being about one-fifth of a second, this raises the interesting problem of how one person can read twice as fast as another. If the fixation-time is constant, then the only other variable is the amount of material which a person sees during a fixation. This is borne out by research. When eye movements are photographed and recorded on a moving strip of film it can be shown that good readers do actually see two or three words in a fixation, while poor readers see one word or less per fixation.

This is one argument in favour of tachistoscopic training. In tachistoscopic training words are flashed on the screen for less than one-fifth of a second. This means that the student does not have time to make more than one fixation in order to read the amount of material flashed on the screen. By gradually increasing the amount of material flashed, from one word to two words to three words and so on, it is believed that some students at least will be helped to have a greater span of recognition. This opinion is neither proved nor disproved by research. Some reading instructors still maintain that for some students tachistoscopic training is of use in breaking up mental or subvocal word-by-word reading habits also.

Readers can probably not be made aware of their eye movements. They can be made aware of the necessity of reading faster, but actual control of the eye movements while reading seems to reside mostly in the subconscious.

Eye movements can easily be observed by another person. In fact it is interesting and worthwhile to get the class to choose partners and watch each other's eye movements while reading. This can most easily be done by getting the student doing the reading to hold a book high, at eye level, while he reads the top of the page. The observer faces the reader and looks just over the top of the printed page into the reader's eyes. The short jerky movements and fixations will be readily apparent. When doing this experiment the student will also notice the 'return sweep' as the student reaches the end of a line of print and sweeps his eyes back to the beginning of the next line of print. (See Figure 5.)

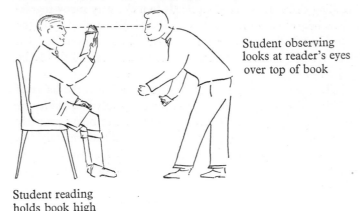

Student observing looks at reader's eyes over top of book

Student reading holds book high

Fig. 6. Students observing eye movements.

REGRESSIONS

One more reading fault the students might see while observing another reading or become conscious of in their own reading is the making of 'regressions'. A regression is a backward movement along a line of print. This means that the student is re-reading a word or phrase. It is easily distinguished from the return sweep, which is usually much longer. Sometimes a regression will take the form of going back over a word or phrase several times before going on to the next part of the line. In a general way, regressions are a sign of poor reading. All readers make some regressions, but good readers make very few, and bad readers make a large number.

Sometimes a regression means that the reader has come across a new word or phrase which he does not quite understand and wishes to review. Making a regression for this purpose is justifiable. But poor readers have a *habit* of making regressions and tend to make many more than they need. You should instruct the class *never* to make regressions while doing reading drill. If the student needs to make very many regressions because of difficult phrases or difficult vocabulary in the reading-speed exercise, then the material of the exercise is on the wrong level for that student and easier material should be selected.

The most common fault among poor readers is the habitual making of too many regressions. Possibly this bad habit was started by the student's reading material not being properly graded for him. Forcing him to read too difficult material has engendered the habit of making regressions. To cure this habit the student should be given ample amounts of easy reading.

EASY READING PRACTICE

Easy reading material, such as adapted classics and specially prepared material with controlled vocabulary and sentence-structure, will not harm anyone and is a great help to poor readers. It helps them in establishing reading patterns of ease and fluency while giving them the wonderful experience of enjoying reading without having to struggle with unfamiliar words and difficult phrases.

In fact, alongside this course, teachers should try to arrange the students' outside study so that they do as much easy reading as possible. This might call for the postponement of reading in difficult set-books for several weeks while the course is being taken. In the long run this could be a more efficient procedure, as the student would be better able to read difficult material at the conclusion of the course. During the course the students should be encouraged to read as much easy material as possible or even have some set for homework.

This easy reading material should often take the form of

novels of moderate length so that the student, by getting engrossed in the reading, will carry on for longer than the extent of a short story. He could also have the satisfaction of finishing

EASY READING

TALE OF TWO CITIES

Date	Pages Read	Time Spent
23/2	1–25	¾ hr.
25/2	26–59	1 hr
26/2	60–72	20 min.
27/2	73–97	¾ hr.
2/3	98–112	20 min
3/3	. 113–156	1 hr

TWO YEARS BEFORE THE MAST

Date	Pages Read	Time Spent
21/5	1–16	20 min
22/5	17–40	40 min
23/5	41–62	¾ hr.
24/5	63–82	30 min

Fig. 7. Student's record of easy reading.

a book or two a week if the books were not too long. There is a large number of adapted and easy novels available for this purpose. This is not an argument that students should *always* read easy and adapted novels; rather it is a strong suggestion that during this course the student do as much *easy* reading as possible. It will help both his speed and comprehension in all types of reading later on. If the students keep a record of their easy reading, the teacher can check on their progress by looking at this while the class does comprehension questions from the *Drill Book*.

HOMEWORK

Finally the teacher should remind the student of the importance of doing homework diligently, and trying to improve both speed and comprehension. As the famous American psychologist Edward Thorndike found years ago, mere repetition or practice without trying to improve yields no learning at all. The student is losing much of the value of the exercise if he simply does a timed reading drill, followed by the comprehension test, in a very relaxed manner. It is only through his efforts to improve that improvement in the reading process occurs. If the teacher is following the plan put forward in this book, one exercise of a timed reading passage followed by comprehension questions will be done in class each week, while two exercises are done for homework each week in addition to easy reading done voluntarily or as set.

CLASS DRILL

The timed reading passages given in class should usually be marked by the students themselves. As we shall see in the next chapter, this not only provides better training for the student through his understanding immediately how well he has done; it also frees the teacher from the drudgery of correcting papers. Teachers have more important things to do than correcting papers that can be marked by the pupil. The teacher can best use the time by helping weak students. He should remember to keep a class record of progress as shown in Fig. 4.

The timing of the drill given in class is the same as that described in chapter 1 for the initial reading test. Before starting the timing the teacher should give the students a short talk to encourage them to try to read a little faster.

While the students are working on their comprehension tests and marking their own papers, the teacher might be computing the class averages from the preceding week. An improving class average is a further encouragement.

After the students have corrected their own tests, the teacher can read the roll and each student can give aloud his speed and comprehension score, while the teacher writes down the scores. This tends to give each student a little recognition and saves the teacher the time used in recording scores by looking through the books or papers of the whole class.

SUMMARY AND SUGGESTED LECTURE OUTLINE

1. Reading is mental and not physical activity.
2. Readers should not point at words.
3. Readers should not move their heads.
4. Readers should not vocalize.
5. Readers should not subvocalize.
6. Students should cure subvocalization by thinking about the material. Emphasize *understanding* and *speed*.
7. Good readers have a larger span of recognition.
8. Students might observe each other's eye movements, noting fixations, return sweeps and regressions.
9. Readers must avoid regressions.
10. Easy reading practice should be given for homework.
11. Two timed reading passages might be set as homework.
12. Students should do homework with diligence.
13. The teacher should encourage the students to correct their own work in the class-drill.

3

COMPREHENSION

It is very difficult to define reading comprehension. Reduced to its simplest elements we might say that comprehension is a part of the communication process of getting the thoughts that were in the author's mind into the reader's mind. This is a difficult process, because it involves the transmission of an idea through several imperfect media. For example, the author must first have a clear idea in his mind, then reduce this idea to written language; this will be printed; and finally the reader looks at the printed word and forms an idea.

A basic assumption is that the writer and the reader speak the same language. If a writer wishes to transmit the idea of 'a cow', he writes the word *cow*. He is assuming that the reader also uses the word *cow* to mean the idea of 'cow' rather than some other word such as *vaca*, which would be used by a Spaniard. Minor but important variations occur even between speakers of the same language, because of the individual's background. For example, *cow* might mean to one person a big terrifying animal with horns, while another person might associate the word *cow* with a kindly milk-giving creature that moos softly.

COMPREHENSION A PART OF COMMUNICATION

If we look at Fig. 8 we can see some of the sources of error in the communication process. First of all the author has selected a word which does not exactly describe the idea which was in his mind. He chose the word *cow* when perhaps he

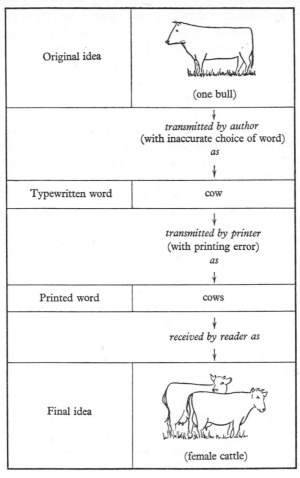

Original idea	(one bull)
	transmitted by author (with inaccurate choice of word) *as*
Typewritten word	cow
	transmitted by printer (with printing error) *as*
Printed word	cows
	received by reader as
Final idea	(female cattle)

Note: Author's slightly inaccurate choice of word, printer's error and reader's assumption.

Fig. 8. Communication problems.

should have used the words *a bull*. When the writer's manuscript was submitted to the printer another error crept in when the printer accidentally put an *s* on the end of the word *cow*. The reader now seeing the word *cows* reacted according to his knowledge of the language and got the idea of two or more female cattle.

While printers' errors might be considered a very minor source of inaccuracy in transmission, there is a real problem involved in the author's selection of words. Written language is a wonderful medium of communication but it is not always as accurate as a writer needs. Skill in using the language also varies considerably. From the standpoint of the reader it is always difficult to know exactly what the author means by the words you see on the page. Children and students for whom English is a second language have further difficulty in that they do not even know the generally agreed (i.e. 'dictionary') meanings of many words. To learn a language, even one's own, it is necessary to know some of the cultural background, and the way that the words are used. Dictionaries can help, but wide reading and living experience of the language are the best method of understanding how to use it.

In teaching reading comprehension the teacher must always keep in mind that the goal is to understand what the author meant.

OBJECTIVE AND SUBJECTIVE COMPREHENSION

Reading can usually conveniently be thought of as being on two levels at once. First the reader should *get the objective facts*. If the story says that 'there were two cows' the reader should get the idea that 'there were two cows'. This is a fact, and requires little interpretation or judgement.

On a higher level the reader should also *get the subjective information*. This subjective information might include such things as the tone and mood of the story. It might only hint at other situations with which the reader is supposed to be familiar. Or the reader might be expected to generalize from the specific facts given, in order to get a main idea which is not specifically stated. For example, the author might not say 'this is a sad story', but the student should be able to get the idea from the choice of words and total situation. Or in another example the author might quote statistics on the number of people killed, the way in which they were killed, and the physical disability of the people who were almost killed, in order that the reader should get the underlying theme that war is a horrible process.

Often authors do not or cannot state the main purpose of an article. It is for the reader to bring his own background knowledge and thinking ability to bear in order to get the main idea. Readers who can only read facts and nothing more can never be called good readers. On the other hand, readers who cannot get the facts seldom get the subjective points.

COMPREHENSION DRILL IN THE 'DRILL BOOK'

There are ten questions following each timed reading passage. These are there because the students must learn that every time they read they must understand. Usually there is no point in reading at any speed, unless they can demonstrate that they have understood. The questions are roughly divided into two types of comprehension. The first half of the questions are more or less objective, that is, they require understanding of specifically stated facts. The second half of the questions tend to require a more subjective type of comprehension. These are questions of generalization, mood or tone, and logical assumptions that can be drawn from the reading passage.

There may at times be disagreement between the student's opinion and the 'correct' answer as given in the answer key for the subjective questions. But simply because the questions are subjective it is difficult to have an absolutely 'correct' answer.

It is often a matter of opinion which answer is correct, and at times a useful class discussion can centre on the choice of answer. The important thing for the teacher to keep in mind is that the exact answer to the question is far less important than the fact that the students are being made aware of the subjective side of reading comprehension. If the students understand the story well enough to argue with the key, this is a healthy sign.

IMPROVING LOW COMPREHENSION

Students can be made aware of their comprehension faults by making them analyse their wrong answer after taking a test. The students should be instructed to re-read carefully each question for which they gave a wrong answer, then to turn to the story and see if they can find the place where the correct answer is given. An exact spot in the story can often be found answering the objective questions, but to find the justice of the correct answers to subjective questions may require that the student glance over the entire story and then think about it a little.

Useful comprehension lessons can be conducted by the teacher for the entire class by making students read aloud individual questions and discuss the answers. Wrong answers might be read aloud as well as right ones, as sometimes useful discussion can follow, telling why a particular answer is wrong.

Teachers can also help comprehension and build up vocabulary by discussing the meanings of some of the more difficult words used in the story. A dictionary, encyclopaedia or other reference book might be used by the student to clarify and expand the meanings of some of the words used in the stories and questions. Since the subject-matter of the stories in the *Drill Book* is related to public health, it might be well to tie the reading drill to a biology or health lesson.

A. *Study the question carefully. You may have not read it correctly.*

Example:

5. The island monkeys served the doctor by:
   (a) bringing him tea,
   (b) allowing themselves to be caught,
   (c) catching other monkeys, or
   (d) sitting in wire cages in trees.

The correct answer is (d) but the student's answer was (b). On re-reading the question carefully after knowing that his choice was wrong he might see that while it is true that the monkeys were caught it is highly doubtful that they would allow themselves to be caught. The other two answers, (a) and (c), are also obviously wrong.

B. *Look for the correct answer in the story for objective questions.*

Example:

1. Dr Causey's reputation as a monkey catcher was:
   (a) poor,   (b) average,
   (c) good, or   (d) the best in the world.

The student chose (b) which was wrong. By looking back in the story the student found the following sentence in the middle of the first paragraph: 'Dr Causey was very good at catching these animals.' Hence the student can see that (c) was the best answer choice and also that the answer was specifically given in the middle of a paragraph. Hence he must read a little more carefully in the future.

C. *Glance over entire story and think about it for subjective questions.*

Example:

9. From reading this article you would judge that Dr Causey is really interested in:
   (a) monkeys,   (b) world health,
   (c) jungles,   (d) adventure.

The student chose (a) because most of the article was about monkeys. While it is true that the doctor did work with monkeys and probably had some interest in them, was this really his main interest? Probably each of the answers was partly correct. The student might have to reason that the doctor used monkeys to expose them to disease, to get blood samples, to analyse these blood samples, to find viruses, to advance medical science, to help people's health everywhere. Hence the correct answer is (b), 'world health', even though nowhere in the story does it say 'the doctor is really interested in world health'.

Fig. 9. Improvement of low comprehension by study of wrong answers.

IMPORTANCE OF SELF-CORRECTION

It is a good teaching method to make the students correct their own papers immediately after taking the comprehension test. The more immediate the knowledge of right or wrong, the better the learning. Students will receive a certain satisfaction from knowing that they got the questions correct. If the questions were answered wrongly, they should know this as soon as possible so that they can correct their errors.

Making the students correct their own papers immediately after a test is much better than taking their papers away, correcting them, and returning them some 24 hours or more later. The teacher may have to correct test papers where he wants an accurate assessment of the students' progress; but if the purpose of the drill is the student's learning reading comprehension, then let him correct his own papers. In some schools there is too much emphasis on testing and too little emphasis on learning.

FEEDBACK TO TEACHER

This process of the student's correcting his own papers immediately, so that he knows the correctness of his responses, is called 'feedback'. Feedback helps learning and the more of it there is the better. A student who persists in making the wrong response and is never told will not learn the right response. But just as the student must have feedback for his responses in a learning situation, the teacher must have feedback for his responses in a teaching situation. This means that the teacher must know whether the student is learning or not, so that he can continue the lessons in the same manner, or change or stop them. Feedback comes to the teacher in many forms: test results, oral responses in class, the look on a student's face, or seeing that the student has the ability to use the skill in a different situation.

The teacher can have excellent feedback in a reading course because of the frequent scores available for both comprehension and reading speed. This is why he should keep a class record and class average of the weekly class-drill. The record will show which students are progressing and which are failing to progress. It will also show which students are weak in comprehension and which are weak in speed.

More accurate information can sometimes be had by looking at the students' answers for several exercises. For example, if a student is consistently getting low comprehension scores a glance at the individual answers of his last few comprehension tests may show that he is doing quite well in the objective factual questions but very poorly in the subjective questions.

By working out the class average each week in both speed and comprehension the teacher knows whether or not the class as a whole is progressing satisfactorily. But the progress of the class average should not cause the teacher to neglect individual marks, because there will usually be a few students who are lagging behind the class. Sometimes it will be found that these are not doing their homework, or that they are unenthusiastic, or it may be that perhaps they are failing to analyse their wrong answers by looking back at the story.

Progress charts should be kept by each individual student. There is a place at the back of the *Drill Book* for recording on separate charts the reading speed and reading comprehension of each class-drill. Each week when the student completes his exercise in class, after marking it, he should write his score in both the speed graph and the comprehension graph. It is easier for the student and the teacher to see progress by looking at a graph than at a string of numbers. The graphs, especially when the curve is rising, often provide real encouragement for the student. They also show such reading faults as a gradual

31

drop in reading comprehension, which would be likely to go unobserved if the only record was numerical scores scattered through the book.

HIGH COMPREHENSION

The level of comprehension is an important factor which both teacher and student must keep constantly in mind. Normal comprehension for the type of exercise given in the *Drill Book* is roughly 70%. This means that we might normally expect the class average to be 70% on a reading exercise done in class. It also means that an average efficient reader should have comprehension scores which hover in the neighbourhood of 70%. If a student scores 80% this means that he is comprehending slightly more than average, and this is all to the good.

If the student consistently scores 90 or 100% on the comprehension test it may mean that he is paying too much attention to comprehension and too little to speed. Very often students who score 90 or 100% consistently in comprehension drill have extremely low reading speeds. Even if their reading speed is within the normal range of the class, very high comprehension scores mean that the student has the ability to go much faster. It is often a far more efficient reading procedure to read 400 words per minute with 70% comprehension than 200 words per minute with 90% comprehension. If for some reason it is important that the student be able to comprehend 100% of the material, then a 'study technique', which will be discussed in a later chapter, is a better procedure than ordinary reading.

It is not necessary for students to get 100% on most of their reading. For newspapers, reports and magazine articles 100% comprehension is seldom appropriate. Moreover, ordinary English prose usually has a certain element of redundancy, that is, the author says the same thing more than once, usually in slightly different ways, simply because he realizes that the reader does not usually have 100% comprehension. So explain to the few students who consistently have comprehension scores that are 'too high' that it is better for them to read faster so that they can cover more material. If *after* the student has learned how to read faster he wishes to slow down so that his comprehension will be nearer 100%, this is another matter. But most often the teacher will find that students who are poor readers have no flexibility in reading and cannot read fast even if they need to. It is one of the intentions of this reading course that the teacher should show the students how to be flexible in their reading so that they may go faster and perhaps lose a little comprehension when they want to. This is not to say that they will always want to read at top speed. Certainly from the standpoint of doing the exercises in the *Drill Book* there is no particular value in having 100% comprehension on every exercise.

A rough measure of 'reading efficiency' might be found by multiplying speed by comprehension.

Perfect comprehension	Poor comprehension
200 w.p.m.	200 w.p.m.
100 % comp.	50 % comp.
= 200 w.p.m. efficiency	= 100 w.p.m. efficiency

Usually a high comprehension means that the student could read much faster with only a small drop in comprehension. This would increase efficiency.

200 w.p.m.	375 w.p.m.
90 % comp.	70 % comp.
= 180 w.p.m. efficiency	= 262 w.p.m. efficiency

Table 2. 'Reading efficiency'. (High comprehension is not required in most reading—getting the main ideas and some of the facts is enough. The English used in newspapers and magazines is 50% redundant: this means that half the ideas, usually the main ones, are repeated.)

33

Far more frequent will be the problem of the student with comprehension which is too low. First let us point out that a comprehension score of 20 or 30 in a test such as is used in the *Drill Book*, which uses four-choice questions, means nothing. By simply not reading the question and guessing at the answer an average chance score of 25% would be obtained. Hence if a student consistently scores 20 or 30% it means that he may not be comprehending anything. He could get the same scores by simply writing down 'a', 'b', 'c' or 'd' without reading the question.

A student who consistently scores 50% is understanding something, but this score is unsatisfactory for most exercises.

One of the most important things the teacher can do is to get the students to balance their reading speed and comprehension. It has long been a myth that fast readers comprehend less. A look at your first week's test results will quickly show that this is not the case. In fact there is usually little relationship between speed and comprehension. This means that some fast readers have poor comprehension and some fast readers have good comprehension. The same is true of the slow readers. But an interesting phenomenon which does occur is that when an individual student first increases his reading speed it is quite frequently accompanied by a drop in comprehension. When this occurs to an individual, the teacher should tell him to 'level off' his reading speed. This means keeping the reading speed at its new high rate, rather than going back to the earlier reading speed, but trying to bring comprehension up to normal. For example, if at the beginning of the course a student is reading at 150 words per minute with 70% comprehension, and at the end of the third week he is reading 200 words per minute with 50% comprehension, the teacher should tell him to continue reading at 200 words per minute but to try to bring his compre-

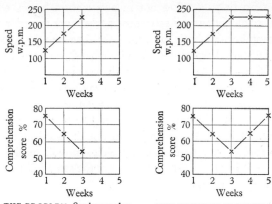

THE PROBLEM: Student makes
rapid speed increase
but loses comprehension.

THE CORRECT SOLUTION:
Level off speed increase
and concentrate on improving
comprehension.

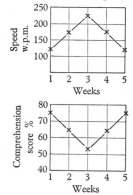

THE WRONG SOLUTION: It is wrong to lower speed
(lose the gain) in order to raise comprehension.

Note: In the wrong solution the student has exactly the same
speed and comprehension at the fifth week as he did at the first
week; hence no improvement has taken place.

Fig. 10. Graphs showing the right and wrong way
to get comprehension back to normal.

hension up to 70%. Do not in any circumstances tell the student to slow down to 150 words per minute in order to get his comprehension back to normal, for then he will be exactly where he started from. On the other hand, do not encourage the student to keep increasing his speed before his comprehension has returned to a normal level. Some students or teachers are apt to be frightened when they see this first comprehension drop which has accompanied a sudden speed increase. It is the teacher's job to tell the student that this often happens, and that his comprehension will surely return to normal if he will continue reading at the same increased rate but not trying to increase it further.

BALANCING SPEED AND COMPREHENSION

Balancing these variations between reading speed and comprehension scores is one of the most important tasks for both teacher and student during this reading course. This is why individual reading and comprehension graphs must be kept by the student so that both he and the teacher may glance at the graphs and quickly see whether speed or comprehension should be emphasized next.

SUMMARY AND SUGGESTED LECTURE OUTLINE

1. Reading comprehension is part of the communication process between two people (see Fig. 8, p. 25).
2. Comprehension is of several kinds:
   (*a*) Objective information—facts.
   (*b*) Subjective information which includes moods, unstated ideas, the overall idea.
3. The test questions are half objective and half subjective.

4. Improve low comprehension by:

(*a*) Making students study questions they failed to get right, looking up the answers in the story.

(*b*) Class discussions of right and wrong answers.

(*c*) Discussions of vocabulary.

5. Immediate self-correction helps learning.

6. Knowing 'why answers are wrong' also helps.

7. Feedback to the teacher helps teaching.

8. Speed and comprehension records help both student and teacher. Progress charts should be kept.

9. Comprehension that is very high (90%) usually means speed is too low.

10. Aim at a balance of speed and comprehension.

11. Aim at flexibility.

12. If a rapid speed increase is accompanied by a comprehension drop, hold the speed score constant and raise comprehension (see Fig. 10, p. 35). *Do not* lower speed.

(If the teacher is following the plan suggested in this book, one class exercise is done each week and two similar exercises are to be done at home. Extra easy reading is also encouraged or set.)

4

UNITS OF MEANING

In the last chapter we saw that reading comprehension was part of the process of getting the idea from the author's mind into the student's mind. Students of modern educational psychology will recognize some of the ideas in that chapter as coming from communication or information theory. In this chapter we shall endeavour to understand reading from the standpoint of the reader perceiving meaningful units. Some readers will recognize this as an application of *gestalt* psychology.

LETTERS AS UNITS OF MEANING

The reader is presented with a page of printed matter, such as that at which you are now looking. How does he perceive it so that he gets the idea from it? Surely he simply does not look at the page as a whole to see if margins are neat and the words arranged in straight lines. No, obviously he must look at some smaller unit. For example, let us assume that the reader is presented with this sample sentence:

The old black dog ran and bit the boy.

If we begin examining this sentence in its smallest units we see that it is composed of letters of the alphabet. By definition, an alphabetical letter is a symbol which stands for a speech-sound. If we had a perfectly phonetic language, which we have not, each letter would stand for a speech-sound and each speech-sound would have a letter. If we take the first word, *the*, and we examine the first letter of this word, *t*, we might remember that the *t* stands for the '*t* sound' as seen at the

38

beginning of the words *top* or *toy*. This is a useful bit of information but unfortunately in this case it is not complete, because the two letters *th* are a digraph and must be seen as one unit in order to get the proper speech-sound. This is usually the '*th* sound' as heard at the beginning of the word *this*. So even to get the right speech-sound we must sometimes see letters in combinations and not as single letters.

WORDS AS UNITS OF MEANING

It is obviously senseless to look for meaning, or the idea in the author's mind, by examining individual letters. The idea is not contained in the individual letter, so there is no point in

---

the
t = *t* sound in *top*
      but
th = *th* sound in *this*
      (so don't always stop at individual letters)
the = a word, but of little meaning
the dog = a particular dog, different from 'a dog'.
Hence meaning is in larger group, not smallest unit.

Fig. 11. Analysis of a word.

studying it further. Let us then take a slightly larger meaningful unit, namely, the entire first word *the*. If we see the letters *t, h, e* placed together in that particular order they form a meaning-unit, a word. If we then ask what is the meaning of the word *the* we have a relevant question, but unfortunately not one that is easy to answer. *The* is an article; more than that, it is the definite article; '*the* dog' is different from 'a dog'. *The* contributes towards the meaning; but by itself *the* has almost no meaning.

Perhaps it is not fair to study a word like *the*; we should take a more basic word such as *dog*. Again if we look closely at *dog* we see that *d* by itself means nothing but a speech-sound, but

4-2

when *d*, *o*, *g* are placed in that particular relationship to each other, one understands the concept of 'dog'. If the same letters are arranged in any other order, for example *god*, we see that they have quite another meaning. Hence not only the particular letters of the alphabet are important, but also the order in which they are arranged.

WRITING IS A DOUBLE ABSTRACTION

Another interesting aspect of reading is the 'double abstraction' concept. The letters of a word stand for a sound. And the sound in turn stands for the idea. The letters *dog* represent the sound a speaker makes when he pronounces the word out loud. But when a speaker says the word 'dog' he is making a noise which in no way resembles a dog. If the speaker said 'bow-wow' he would at least be making a noise which had a direct relationship to a dog. But when he makes the sound 'dog' he is using the sound as a complete abstraction, namely, the sound that he makes with his mouth when he says 'dog' is simply a *sound-symbol* that stands for an idea. When the word *dog* is printed on a page another system of symbols is being used: the system of alphabet symbols, which as we have already seen are a set of symbols which stand for speech-sounds.

Hence,

a printed word is a group of visual symbols →
which stand for a speech-symbol →
which stands for an idea.

When one thinks about the complexity of the psychological task involved in reading, it is a wonder that so many children learn to read satisfactorily at all.

DROP SOUND ABSTRACTIONS

We stated in an earlier chapter that subvocalization, or internally saying the words to oneself, was not an efficient practice. Now perhaps the reason for this is clear. In reading, the reader is dealing with *two* sets of abstractions. Efficient readers are able simply to look at the printed symbol and get the idea directly without going through the sound stage. It is a useful crutch for most beginning readers to look at the printed symbol, translate this into the sound- or speech-symbol, and then get the idea. But mature readers do not need to go through this sound stage, they may go directly from the printed word to the concept. In other words the mature reader may look at the symbols *dog* and get the idea 'dog' without going through the intermediate stage of saying the word 'dog' to himself.

The main point of this is to make the reader grasp that he should go as directly as possible to the author's idea. He should not be a proof-reader and worry about spelling, he should not be a radio announcer and worry about pronunciation, he should be a mind-reader and try to determine quickly and efficiently what the author had in mind.

There is disagreement among psychologists as to the nature of thought. Some feel that thought is heavily dependent on a type of subvocalization while others feel that much thought is of a non-vocal nature. There is no need in this discussion to take sides in that argument: it is more important to emphasize the difference between oral reading and silent reading. It is an undisputed fact that efficient readers can read much faster silently than aloud, and it is our goal to teach students to read silently, faster and more efficiently.

PHRASE AS A UNIT OF MEANING

Now back to our analysis of the sentence:

The old black dog ran and bit the boy.

We have seen that the idea that the author is trying to convey to the reader is certainly not contained in the individual letters, nor, in some instances at least, in the single whole word. We have seen that some words, such as *dog*, have 'more' meaning than other words, such as *the*. If we look at some of the other words in the sentence such as *old* and *black* we see that these are interesting words but hardly have complete meaning by themselves. The word *black* is a vague concept. It is true that black is a colour, but the author is not trying to give us the idea of 'blackness'. He is simply trying to tell us about an animal which is not just 'a dog' but a particular dog, namely '*the* dog'. Furthermore, this dog cannot be confused with many other dogs because he is 'black' and he is 'old'. So that the reader cannot take any of the first four words by themselves. *The* and *old* and *black* by themselves have little meaning. Even the word *dog*, while it has more meaning and can stand alone, is still not as meaningful as when it is seen in relationship to *the old black*. Hence, in order to get the meaning that the author intended, the reader must perceive *the old black dog* as one unit.

'Perception' is not the same thing as eye movements. Perception here is a mental or psychological phenomenon, and whether the reader sees the four words in one fixation, or two or three, is not as important as his mental process, which would perceive them as a meaningful group.

SENTENCE AS A UNIT MEANING

Now what is the author trying to convey to the reader? Is he simply trying to convey the notion that 'the old black dog' exists? No, he is trying to convey to the reader a much larger and more complex idea, namely 'the old black dog is *running* and he is *biting* the *boy*'. In other words the author has in his mind a concept of an old black dog running and biting a boy. He wishes to tell us that a particular action took place between this dog and a certain boy. Thus the author is trying to give us a *complete thought*. Sometimes English teachers explain a sentence as being composed of a subject and predicate. But a psychologist would be more happy with the teacher's definition of a sentence as a complete thought.

42

Sometimes psychologists refer to these units of meaning as *gestalts*. Gestalt is a German word which means organization or whole or pattern. Thus a word is a gestalt, a phrase such as 'the old black dog' is a larger unit of meaning or larger gestalt. The whole sentence, 'the old black dog ran and bit the boy', is an even larger meaning-unit or gestalt. The teacher will be able to extend this idea quickly to where a definition of a paragraph is simply a larger unit of meaning or larger gestalt. In the same sense a chapter or unit of a book is also a gestalt.

What the gestalt psychologist is telling us is that man's mind works in terms of meaning-units. Certainly psychologists did not invent the idea of writing in words or sentences or paragraphs; but rather words and sentences and paragraphs are organized in written and oral communication because this is the way man's mind works. If the reader understands this, he will know where to look for the meaning in a written work. He will not look at the individual letter for meaning. He will not look at the individual word for meaning. He will look at the inter-relationship of words in such units as phrases and sentences and paragraphs. By themselves very few words contain enough meaning to be worthwhile. It is the way words are used in relationship to each other which contains meaning.

LOOK FOR LARGER UNITS

Slow readers who read one-word-at-a-time often have great difficulty in getting meaning from a printed page, simply because they are looking in the wrong spot. They are perceiving single words as single words. And a mature reader can never get the meaning from written material simply by looking at single words. The meaning is simply not contained in individual words. This is one reason why fast readers are often superior readers. They perceive words as groups. Their minds are set on getting the meaning out of the inter-relationship between the words. If students insist on slowly reading and saying each word to themselves, they are placing their mental emphasis in the wrong place.

Subvocalization is bad because, as we saw, meaning is not contained in the sound symbol. Pronouncing words aloud while reading is only a crutch to help the very immature who have a better speaking than reading knowledge of the language.

Some readers are 'too close' to the material. They insist on carefully looking at and pronouncing each word in a sentence. If it is a long sentence, by the time they get to the end they have all but forgotten the beginning. Better is the reader who stands back and tries to perceive the sentence as a whole so that he sees the inter-relationship of all the words and phrases. The important thing in reading is for the reader to place his attention where it should be: on trying to get the ideas.

LARGER UNITS REQUIRE MATURITY

The younger the reader or the more immature the reader, the smaller the gestalt that he can handle. This means that young children and beginning readers have difficulty in seeing meaning, or perceiving larger patterns as wholes. This is why beginning reading material does and should have small sentences. It is easier for a beginning reader to see four or five words as a meaningful whole, such as might be found in a short simple sentence, than it is for him to see the overall pattern of a twenty-five to fifty-word sentence. College textbooks frequently have fifty-word sentences and some secondary reading material has many sentences longer than twenty-five words. Sentences approaching these lengths have many subordinate clauses and prepositional phrases and so on, which are in themselves small gestalts which add up to a larger gestalt.

44

The ability of the student to handle larger and more complex sentence-patterns is based on two things: his native intelligence, and past learning. While the teacher can do little about his native intelligence, it is the primary purpose of the teaching profession to deal with learning. One way in which the student learns to handle larger and larger sentence-patterns is by experience. This is why it is important for him to do as much

---

The large grey house that the farmer lived in has been sold to the soldier who was here last summer.

There is a large grey house.
A farmer lived in it.
The house has been sold.
A soldier bought it.
The soldier was here last summer.

Fig. 12. Large and small gestalts in sentences.

easy reading as possible, so that he can become familiar with the simple and fairly simple types of sentence-patterns that are used in English writing. It is only when the simple and fairly simple patterns or sentences have been mastered that the student should be made or expected to struggle through, learn, and master the more complex sentences which are used in adult written material.

In Fig. 12 we see an example of a large gestalt in one sentence which can subsequently be broken down into a number of smaller gestalts. The teacher will recognize that the first sentence is fairly complex, with a number of clauses such as might be found in material for mature readers. Beneath that, the same number of ideas has been broken down into small short sentences such as might be found in a beginning readers' book.

The reason why one long sentence is used for mature readers, and the short choppy sentences for beginning readers, is that the mature reader has the ability to form larger gestalts. He is familiar with the handling of the phrases and it is not necessary for the author to break them down into small simple gestalts for him. Not only this, but the large sentences contain some subtle inter-relationships which are difficult to express by the short choppy sentences. The large sentence has a certain flow and unity which short choppy sentences have not. By and large, the short sentences convey the main pieces of information that the author wishes to transmit, but the author knows that mature readers like their information in larger meaningful units. In teaching reading comprehension the instructor should take large sentences and show what information they contain. Then the student must have adequate practice in reading both small and large sentences if he is to have facility in handling larger gestalts which are used in more mature reading.

SUMMARY AND SUGGESTED LECTURE OUTLINE

1. Examine the sentence 'The old black dog ran and bit the boy'.
2. Meaning is not contained in single letters.
3. Single words have little meaning.
4. Writing is a double abstraction. Letter-symbols represent sound-symbols, which represent the concept.
5. Good readers drop the sound-symbol (i.e. don't subvocalize) and go direct from the printed word to the concept.
6. The phrase has more meaning than single words.
7. The sentence is a most important unit of meaning.

8. Units of meaning are called gestalts, and increase in size from word, to phrase, to sentence, to paragraph, to chapter. This is how the mind works.

9. Look for meaning in larger units of written material.

10. Reading larger units requires maturity.

11. Students should improve their reading by starting with smaller units; i.e. get a lot of practice on easy reading matter.

12. Show how complex sentences contain smaller meaningful units (see Fig. 12, p. 45).

13. Complex sentences have better style for mature readers.

5

SKIMMING AND READING FLEXIBILITY

So far we have talked about reading as though it were a single process. We talked about increasing reading speed as though a person had only one speed and once this was increased all his reading would be done at this increased speed. Unfortunately, reading speed is not so simple. There are many kinds of reading speed, which depend on the difficulty of the material being read as well as the student's own reading ability and background knowledge.

In order to simplify the subject, let us state that there are three speeds. The teacher will of course realize that there is no clear distinction between the three different types of reading speed, but they are separated here so that we may study them.

STUDY READING SPEED

The first reading speed we might call 'study speed'. This is the slowest reading speed, and it is used for difficult material. It is also used when one wishes to have a high rate of understanding as well as good retention. In this type of reading the student attempts to study the material carefully so that he will not miss a single point. He also hopes to remember the material at a later time. Unfortunately, many students use this slow study speed when really they should be using a 'study technique'. Study techniques involve such things as reading the material once rapidly then going back over it to pick up more of the details, or underlining, or outlining, or thinking of questions on the material and answering them, and so on. Study techniques will be discussed in a later chapter; often per hour of study they will yield more intensive comprehension and memorization of the material than study reading alone.

There are obvious times when a student must read at study speed, as when he encounters difficult text-books, exact directions to be followed, or legal documents which have a strange phraseology and exacting vocabulary. However, there is one danger in reading difficult material at study speed, and that is this: when a student finds material difficult he slows down; the material is still difficult so he slows down still further. After he has slowed down several times in order to attempt to comprehend the difficult material he may find that he is going so slowly that his comprehension would be improved if he could speed up his reading. In other words, sometimes if a student is having difficulty in understanding very difficult material he will get more out of it by speeding up his reading a little and reading the material twice, or by going over the material once lightly and then coming back and reading at study speed. The danger here is that it is possible to go so slowly that comprehension gets worse instead of better. There is a point beyond which slow reading actually makes comprehension worse, and students are exposed to this risk when they encounter extremely difficult material. Study techniques or double reading will help to save them from this fault.

Reading speed on very difficult material can be increased. An increase in reading speed on material of average difficulty will also increase reading speed on very difficult material. I once gave a reading-improvement course to a group of executive employees in a large factory. The employees made about 100% gain in speed on material of average difficulty but the company psychologist who tested the class both before and at the end of training, using very difficult reading material, also found that they had increases of about 90%. Of course the employee's reading rate in actual words per minute on the difficult material was always slower than on material of average difficulty.

AVERAGE READING SPEED

The second reading speed we shall call average speed. Reading of average speed is what a student does most of the time. Average reading speed would cover easier text-books, novels, newspapers, and so on. This is the reading speed which this course is aiming to improve, and which is required by the exercises in the *Drill Book*. It is difficult to say exactly what average reading speed should be, but the author's experience with courses in the United States suggests that it should certainly be faster than 250 words per minute, while many students can read quite comfortably at 500 words per minute after training. Comprehension at average speed is about 70%. Average reading speed can be used on most prose material, whether factual description or narrative. It cannot be used for poetry, since poetry often packs ideas very closely together and is usually written so that pronouncing the words, at least sub-vocally, is helpful in getting the rhythm and tone of the poem. But for most students, poetry forms only a small part of the vast amount of material to be read.

Average reading speed varies considerably from person to person and from time to time. A good reader's average reading speed might vary from 250 words per minute to 500 words per minute, while a poor reader's average reading speed might vary from 150 to 180 words per minute. Note that the poor reader's speed has little variation; this is one mark of a poor reader. Variations in speed can be caused by unfamiliarity of the subject being read, the reader's motive or intention in reading, and external conditions such as noise or type-size.

Since most of this course is aimed at improving the student's average reading speed, let us go on to the next interesting step.

Skimming is reading at the fastest speed which a person can accomplish. It is used when a reader wishes to cover material in a hurry. It is also used when high comprehension is not required. This does not mean that in skimming a person accepts a ridiculously low standard of comprehension: merely that he will accept a level of comprehension somewhat lower than that which can be obtained at study speed or at average reading speeds.

It is difficult to say exactly how fast skimming should be, but a safe rule of thumb is that it should be twice as fast as the fastest average reading. If, for example, a student begins a reading course at 200 words per minute, it is reasonable to expect that at the end of this course, if the course has been successful and the student has tried hard, he will be reading at 400 words per minute, average speed. Hence we expect this student's skimming to be 800 words per minute or better.

Now, in order that the student shall achieve this tremendously fast rate of skimming, we must ascribe those characteristics of skimming which make it different from average reading. In average reading the student does not skip any material; he covers the entire amount of reading matter. This does not mean that his eyes fixate or stop on every word, but neither does it mean that he can skip any whole sentences or halves of paragraphs. In skimming, however, it is fair to leave out material. Often a reader will leave out half or three-quarters of a paragraph if he feels he has got the main idea. Thus skimming differs from average reading in the fact that readers selectively leave out chunks of material.

Skimming also differs from average reading in that the student intentionally accepts lowered comprehension. In average reading the student attempts to get as good comprehension as he can; this usually means 70 or 80%, as he is not

51

willing to pay the price of slowness in order to get a higher comprehension score. But the student would take as high a comprehension score as he could manage, provided an average reading speed is maintained. In skimming, the student intentionally accepts lowered comprehension. In terms of the type of exercises found in the *Drill Book*, this means that 50% would be a good average skimming comprehension while 60% would be a little better than average.

Speed		Poor reader	Good reader
Slow	*Study reading speed* is used when material is difficult and/or high comprehension is desired	90–125 w.p.m. 80–90 % comp.	200–300 w.p.m. 80–90 % comp.
Average	*Average reading speed* is used for everyday reading of magazines, newspapers and easier text-books	150–180 w.p.m. 70 % comp.	250–500 w.p.m. 70 % comp.
Fast	*Skimming* is used when the highest rate is desired. Comprehension is intentionally lower	Cannot skim	800+ w.p.m. 50 % comp.

Table 3. The three speeds of reading.

If during skimming the student consistently scores 70 or 80% it means that he is not skimming nearly fast enough and should speed up, however fast he was skimming when he got 70%. Conversely, a consistent score of 30 or 40% is too low. Occasionally a student may hit 40% on a skimming exercise, but if he consistently does this it means that he is not doing his skimming correctly or is attempting to go too fast for his reading abilities.

Thus we see emerging some of the characteristics of skimming, such as: (1) an extremely rapid rate, (2) selective, leaving out of parts of the material, and (3) intentional acceptance of a lowered comprehension (50%)—but not one that is too low.

HOW TO SKIM

Now we come to the problem faced by the student who is about to do a skimming exercise. Precisely what does the student do to get going at this extremely fast rate? What material does he leave out?

Let us say that the student wishes to skim a factual article of several thousand words. He should first read the opening paragraph or two at his fastest average rate. That means that he leaves out nothing, but goes at his top reading speed of 300 or 400 words per minute. He reads the whole of the first several paragraphs in order to get started, to get the idea of the story, the setting, a little of the author's style, the tone or mood, and so on. Frequently an author will give an introduction in the first few paragraphs and this will help to give the reader an overall gestalt of the story. But very shortly, if the student is to achieve a skimming rate of 800 words per minute or better, he must begin leaving out material. Hence, on the third or fourth paragraph he reads only the key sentence, struggles to get the main idea of the paragraph, and skips the second half. Perhaps he will read the key sentence and let his eyes jump down through the paragraph, picking up one or two important words, phrases, or numbers.

Sometimes the key sentence will not be found at the first sentence of the paragraph. The student will then have to hunt around a little in the paragraph in order to get either the key sentence or several phrases or sentences which give the main idea of the paragraph. In skimming, the student attempts to get the main idea of every paragraph plus a few of the facts. He cannot hope to pick up all the facts in the story, but he might pick up some of them, some of the proper names, or some of the numbers.

Usually the first paragraph will be read at average speed all the way through. It often contains an introduction or overview of what will be talked about.

Sometimes, however, the second paragraph contains the introduction or overview. In the first paragraph the author might just be 'warming up' or saying something clever to attract attention.

Reading a third paragraph completely might be unnecessary but ... ...
... ...
... ...
... ...
... ...
... ...
... ...
the main idea is usually contained in the opening sentence
... ...
... ... topic sentence ... ...
... ...
... ...
... ...
... ...
... ...
... ...

Besides the first sentence the reader should get some but not all the detail from the rest of the paragraph ... ...
... ...
... ...
... ...
... ...

... ...
... ...
... ...
... ...
... ...
... ...
... ... names ...
... ...
... ... date ... ...
... ...
... ...
... ...

This tells you nothing ...
... ...
... ...
... ...
hence sometimes the main idea is in the middle or at the end of the paragraph.

Some paragraphs merely repeat ideas ... ...
... ...
... ...
... ...

Occasionally the main idea can't be found in the opening sentence. The whole paragraph must then be read.

Then leave out a lot of the next paragraph ... ...
... ...
... ...
... ...
... ... to make up time
... ...
... ...
... ...
... ...

Remember to keep up a very
fast rate

... ...
... ...
... ...
... ... 800 w.p.m.
... ...
... ...
... ...

    Don't be afraid to leave out
half or more of each paragraph
... ...
... ...
... ...
... ...
... ...

    Don't get interested and start
to read everything ... ...
... ...
... ...
... ...
... ...
... ...
... ...
skimming is work ... ...
... ...
... ...
... ...
... ...
... ...

    Lowered comprehension is
expected ... ...
... ...
... ... 50% ... ...
... ...
... ...
... ... not too low
... ...
... ...

    Skimming practice makes it
easier ... ...
... ...
... ...
... ...
... ...
... ...
... ... gain confidence ...
... ...
... ...
... ...
... ...

    Perhaps you won't get any-
thing at all from a few paragraphs ... ...
... ...
... ...
... ...
... ...
... ...
... ... don't worry
... ...
... ...

    Skimming has many uses ...
... ...
... ... reports ...
... ...
... ... newspapers ... ...
... ...
... ... supplementary
... ... text ... ...

    The ending paragraphs
might be read more fully as
often they contain a summary.

    Remember that the import-
ance of skimming is to get only
the author's main ideas at a very
fast speed.

Fig. 13. What a student might see in skimming.

As the student is skimming through the material he may find that he comes to a paragraph midway in the story where he attempts to get the main idea by reading a key sentence, and cannot find one. He may hunt around in the paragraph trying to find the key word or phrase, but he cannot find this either. He may have to read this entire paragraph in order to get its meaning. But having read a paragraph all the way through he must now skim even faster on the next few paragraphs to make up for lost time. (Study Fig. 13 carefully.)

The entire skimming exercise must be done 'against the clock'. That is the student must be trying to go as fast as he possibly can while leaving out large chunks of material. He must be warned against getting interested in the story, as being interested sometimes means that he slows down and reads things more carefully. Skimming is work. It is done when the student has not much time. It is done when the student wishes to cover the material at the fastest possible rate.

SKIMMING EXERCISES

Skimming takes practice. The easy reading which the student has been asked to do in connexion with this course will help him by giving him familiarity with reading material. Skimming first of all assumes that the reader has some such familiarity. Assuming this familiarity, the student now needs practice in skimming.

When readers first try to skim they often achieve speeds little better than their average reading rate. But skimming exercises must be repeated until they reach some established goal such as 800 words per minute.

Those who have difficulty in learning to skim can often be helped by a simple type of exercise that asks them to skim the same article several times in succession. For example if a student tries to skim an article and gets a rate of only 400 words per minute, he should be asked to re-skim the same article and attempt to get up to 800 words per minute. Perhaps on his second try he will get to 600 words per minute. But he should be told to leave out even more material and go faster until he can achieve his goal of 800 words per minute—even if it is on the third or fourth try. Sometimes the student is humorously told to read nothing but the opening sentence and the last

---

1. In teaching skimming, the teacher should set a goal to be reached that is roughly 4 times faster than the student's beginning w.p.m. rate.

Hence, if the class averages 200 w.p.m. a goal of 800 w.p.m. might be set.

2. When the students first try to skim at 800 w.p.m. many of them will go much slower.

They should then be told to re-skim the same article until they reach the goal of 800 w.p.m. (taking the comprehension test only after the 1st skimming).

A student's paper might look like this:

	1st drill	2nd drill	3rd drill
1st skimming	310 w.p.m.	490 w.p.m.	715 w.p.m.
2nd skimming	450 w.p.m.	630 w.p.m.	825 w.p.m.
3rd skimming	675 w.p.m.	910 w.p.m.	
4th skimming	850 w.p.m.		

Note the improvement on the 1st skimming on each successive drill.

Fig. 14. Re-skimming drill.

paragraph. This is, of course, an exaggeration, but it might help to give him the idea that he must leave out material if he is to go rapidly. (Study Fig. 14.)

Skimming drill must, of course, be followed by comprehension tests, because there is no point in reading material at any rate, including the faster skimming rates, if there is no comprehension. Sometimes articles at the end of the *Drill Book* may be used for skimming drill, or articles that have already been read at the beginning of the *Drill Book* may be used for skimming drill. Magazine articles and chapters from supplementary text-books make good material for skimming practice.

If the teacher is trying to get the student up to a rapid skimming rate by making him do repeated skimmings of the same article, he takes the comprehension test only after the first time.

After skimming at 810 *w.p.m.*

The main idea of the article was that you should go very fast and get mostly the central thought for each paragraph. It is suggested that this can usually be found in the first sentence but it could be in a sentence at the middle or end. The first few and the last few paragraphs of the article should be read more carefully.

After re-reading at 325 *w.p.m.*

My first paragraph was essentially correct except that it might have mentioned more about lowered comprehension being expected. It seems that a skimming comprehension should be about 50 % and that if it is much higher the student should skim faster.

Fig. 15. Samples of paragraphs written to check comprehension after skimming and re-reading.

If the student is practising skimming on magazine articles, text-book chapters, or novels, for which there are no regular comprehension tests, the teacher may (1) make up a few simple questions, or (2) ask the student to write a paragraph giving the main points, or (3) have oral questions or class discussion on the passage skimmed.

Another interesting exercise is to make the students skim an article, and then ask them to write a paragraph stating the main ideas plus a few of the details. The students are then asked to read the article at an average reading rate (not leaving out anything but not going at a study rate). After the second reading the students are asked to write a second paragraph stating whether or not they felt that their first paragraph was essentially correct, giving the main ideas correctly if they were wrong before, and in either case adding a few more details. Their reading time should be taken, and a word-per-minute score worked out, for each reading. (See Fig. 15.)

The length of the reading passage may be estimated by finding the average number of words in the first ten lines and multiplying the average number of words per line by the total number of lines read. If the passage is several pages long, the number of words estimated for one page may be multiplied by the total number of pages.

It is well to make students try skimming in class the first time, so that the teacher may give them a certain amount of supervision and encouragement. But there should also be some skimming done as homework, during which the student should be encouraged to skim up to 800 words per minute even if repeated practice on the same article is necessary.

USES OF SKIMMING

It will be found that training in skimming has a good effect on other reading speeds. Often when a student learns to skim rapidly it will help his other levels of reading, such as average reading and study reading. Hence we see that learning to skim has two distinct values. One, it is a useful skill in itself in that there are many times when a student can use skimming to get information from material he otherwise would not read; and two, skimming is a useful exercise to help the other reading speeds.

The usefulness of skimming can be seen in many situations. Sometimes when a student is asked to do supplementary reading for a course, the teacher will set more supplementary reading than the student can really cover at his average or study rate. If he skims the supplementary material (not his basic text-books), he may be pleased and surprised to learn how much of the material he can comprehend at fast skimming rates.

Businesses and governments often require their employees to read a large number of reports. Some of these reports are not directly related to the employee's job, and he has only a general interest in them. Skimming will often satisfy the employee's needs and the employer's demands for this type of report reading. Adults and students often have a desire to be generally informed in such fields as political affairs or cultural developments and yet they have not the time to read much on these subjects. Skimming will often help to keep them informed in their general fields of interest without taking the time that average reading would.

Skimming is quite useful in building up a fund of reference information. If, for example, an employee or a student is instructed to read regularly several journals or reports in a given field, the chances are that not all the articles in the journal or report will be of equal importance. It is often satisfactory if the student or employee knows merely of the existence of the article and perhaps its main idea. At a later time, at a conference or in a class, the person may cite the main idea of the article, and this makes him seem quite well informed. This is not dishonest, as he *is* better informed than another person who has never even heard of the article (perhaps because he reads so slowly that he never got round to it). If one knows of the existence of the article, one can go back and read it more carefully if the need arises.

The person who has the habit of skimming a large amount of material will invariably come across certain articles or parts of books which are of great importance to him. These parts can be read more carefully. But if he had never developed the habit of skimming, the chances are that he would never have come across the important parts or articles.

Professional people, such as doctors, lawyers, engineers, and teachers should all do a large amount of this type of skimming in order to keep abreast of new developments, since there is now so much being printed that one cannot hope to *read* everything in one's field. In order to produce professional people who have the skill and the habit of skimming, teachers must give the necessary training. Biology students should be asked to skim extra text-books and journal articles; political science students should skim not one but several newspapers, as well as magazine articles and extra texts; and so on for the various fields.

There is another useful function of skimming in finding information. Sometimes the purpose of reading is simply to find the answer to a question. With the question in mind, the student skims through the reading material looking for just one thing, the answer. A type of skimming similar to this is used in finding names in a telephone directory or in using an index of a book.

As skimming drill is practised, and skimming skill used for everyday purposes, the student will become more at home with skimming. He will know when he should skim and when he should not. At first he will probably be surprised at the relatively high amount of information he can get by skimming at fast speeds. As he does more, he will gain in confidence.

Skimming is not a skill which should be used at all times, or a type of reading which should replace all average or study reading. But it is a skill which can and should be used in many instances. As the student becomes familiar with the technique he will find where it can be used to his advantage.

SKIMMING HOMEWORK

In order to help the student both to learn to skim and to establish the habit, the teacher should encourage the skimming of entire magazines, or of certain chapters of supplementary text-books. Students must be made to skim for a while until the habit is established. Once the skill is learned it will be valuable throughout life.

One mark of a poor reader is that he has no rapid reading speed. If a reader has only one reading speed it is almost always slow. Good readers have *flexibility* in their reading. They can go fast when they want to and they can go slowly when they want to. It is hoped that students taking this course will develop control over their reading speed rather than allow their reading speed to have control over them.

SUMMARY AND SUGGESTED LECTURE OUTLINE

There are three reading speeds.

1. Study reading is the slowest; it is for difficult material and for instances where high comprehension and high retention are required. Comprehension 80–90%, w.p.m. 200–300.

2. Average reading is used for everyday reading of magazines, books, and easy texts. Comprehension 70%, w.p.m. 250–500.

3. Skimming is the fastest rate, to be used when in a hurry and high comprehension is not required. Comprehension 50%, w.p.m. 800+ (see Table 3, p. 52).

4. Skimming should be twice as fast as the fastest average rate. Suggested rate: 800 w.p.m.

5. Skimming differs from average reading in that (*a*) some material is skipped, and (*b*) a lower comprehension is intentional.

6. Skimming can be used to cover, and get general ideas and a few details from, supplementary texts, reports, and journals. The general idea is often sufficient, but the reader may refer back to any part and read it more carefully.

7. Skimming is a useful skill for students and professional people.

8. Skimming practice is important to establish skill.

9. Some skimming drills should be done in class.

10. Re-skimming is often necessary to get students up to a desired goal. The suggested goal is 800 w.p.m. (See Fig. 14.)

11. Skimming homework should be set. The teacher may make the student skim one homework exercise and read one exercise in the regular (average) manner. Additional skimming practice in a magazine or book should be arranged. Easy reading should be continued.

12. Flexibility should be developed.

6

IMPROVEMENT PATTERNS

There are a number of different patterns which students follow in making reading improvement. Some students will make a steady week-by-week increase while other students make no increase for several weeks and then a sudden spurt forward. No one type of improvement pattern, as opposed to others, is 'normal'. In this chapter we shall examine a number of these different patterns, because it is useful for the teacher to know about them.

The patterns will be of reading-speed improvement unless otherwise stated. It is also assumed that reading comprehension remains at a normal level. As we saw in an earlier chapter, if reading comprehension remains below normal the speed curve should be levelled off until the comprehension curve returns to normal.

Each student should be making a reading-improvement curve. This curve usually represents the results of the weekly class-tests or drill. Some teachers or students may prefer to use a weekly average instead; this means averaging the class-drill with the two homework exercises. In any event, single homework scores should not be included on the graph, as the conditions under which homework is done are usually different from conditions in class.

STEADY IMPROVEMENT PATTERN

Some students make a steady gain each week. This is not universal, as many things contribute towards variations in the rate of gain, but it is quite normal and desirable.

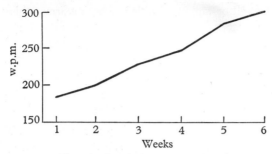

Fig. 16. Steady improvement pattern.

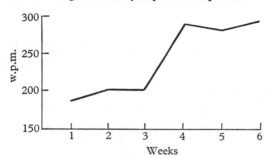

Fig. 17. Sudden improvement pattern.

SUDDEN IMPROVEMENT PATTERN

More interesting, and sometimes more worrying to both the
student and the teacher, is the type of progress which is seen
in the sudden improvement pattern. Here a student might go
on for several weeks making no improvement. Then he
suddenly gets the idea and an upward jump in reading speed
takes place. Sometimes after this sudden increase in speed his
rate will again level off and he will seem to make no improvement for several weeks until again another upward jump is
possible. Educational psychologists call this type of learning
curve an 'insight' curve. They feel that this is characteristic of
a certain type of learning where the student grasps the point

in a sudden, all-or-nothing, fashion. The important thing for the reading teacher and student to remember is that it is quite normal for some students to make no gain for several weeks. If this is not understood the student or teacher could become discouraged at not seeing a steady rate of progress.

In all types of learning it is quite usual to see plateaux. These plateaux are halts in the learning rate: they represent a time when for all measurable purposes no learning is taking place.

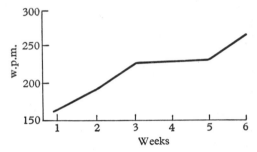

Fig. 18. Plateau pattern.

The learning curve will be seen as a flat line which does not rise. In a plateau pattern a student will make regular gains for several weeks in a row, then hit a period of several weeks in which no increase takes place. As in the 'insight' situation, it is important for the student and teacher not to be discouraged by this halt in progress. It is quite normal for some students to consolidate their gains and to become established and comfortable at the new increased reading rate for several weeks before progressing to higher rates.

When learning a new skill it is not at all unusual for the student to slip back temporarily to earlier and less skilful habits. Some students make far from regular progress in their reading-speed improvement. They will go up one week and down the next. But usually if these students are observed over a period of five or ten weeks it will be seen that on the whole they are making definite improvement. There are a number of things which can cause the reading-improvement curve drop, such as unfamiliarity with the subject of the passage read or slight ill health.

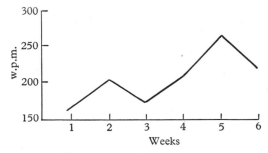

Fig. 19. Irregular progress pattern.

Also a lack of enthusiasm can cause a downward trend; it might be brought on by poor teaching, or by any one of a myriad of emotional factors outside the classroom. In some respects an irregular progress pattern is a good sign, because it means that the student is breaking loose from his old slow, steady habits; out of these irregularities comes the opportunity for learning and establishing newer and better habits.

SMALL IMPROVEMENT PATTERN

In every class there are several pupils who make very little or no reading improvement. Sometimes this is a normal condition and not the fault of poor teaching; but good teachers will have relatively few of these pupils. The course described in this book is designed for students who are in the upper half of the population in terms of learning ability (I.Q.). In places where there is compulsory education and even the duller students are kept at school, such goals as doubling the reading speed can often not be achieved. Where the students are pre-selected (as in the case of those students who are selected for an academic course) this problem of having dull students should be largely eliminated.

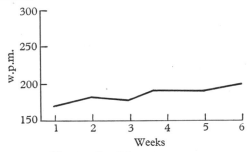

Fig. 20. Small improvement pattern.

I do not mean to say that duller students cannot improve their reading, but merely that the relatively rapid gains described in this book cannot be achieved with slow students. The lower one goes in the intelligence scale, the more difficult it is to increase reading speed and comprehension. This does not mean that a rapid increase in reading speed is always an indication of high intelligence: it is not. Sometimes students with average learning ability only will make satisfactory gains, while students of superior intelligence will make relatively smaller gains. It is possible that some students possess a special talent known as 'reading ability' while other students, gifted in other areas, do not.

It is also possible that in some cases of little or no improvement the student's personality is involved. Some students have the type of personality which is afraid to attempt new things. They may be afraid to let their comprehension fall temporarily for fear that they may never get it back again. Perhaps this is due to a basic insecurity, or to a childhood pattern in which emphasis on perfection, or fear of new things, has been unduly emphasized. Other students seem to be slow, methodical and thorough by nature and the teacher might point out to these students that while these traits are desirable in many occupations they are not always desirable in gaining reading efficiency. Sometimes discussing the importance of flexibility in reading will help this type of student.

HELPING STUDENTS WHO DO NOT IMPROVE

There are several things a teacher can do to help the student who has not shown any speed increase after four or five weeks of training.

Often a greater emphasis on skimming exercises will assist this type of student. If he learns to skim with confidence and a fair degree of comprehension his regular reading habits will often benefit.

Sometimes telling the student without reading improvement to let his comprehension drop can be very helpful. Some students are worried so much about maintaining their comprehension that they are not able to put any emphasis on speed. The teacher should explain to this type of student that these reading exercises are for the purpose of helping reading speed. It is not important that he understand the subject-matter, as in a regular text-book. If a student improves his reading speed it is all that can be desired from this course. Hence one step in improving reading is to let comprehension sink while speed is increased. After speed has been increased the emphasis can be put on comprehension, so that he can achieve a normal balance between comprehension and speed.

Another thing that might be done with students who show

little or no improvement in speed is to ask them to re-read the same article several times. Each time they should try to increase their speed. A watch might be used in this type of drill, and the student asked to report his time after one reading. He should then take the regular comprehension test. The second time, the student reads the article trying to improve his reading rate. He does not take the comprehension test after the second reading. The student should re-read the passage a third time, trying to improve his speed even more. Three readings of one article are usually enough but half a dozen or more exercises of this type in one week are useful. The student might re-read the articles that have been set earlier, reading each one three times and trying to improve his speed with each reading.

Tachistoscopic drill is sometimes helpful for this type of student. Words and phrases can be flashed on a screen with a regular tachistoscope, or 'flash cards' may be used which show words and phrases of gradually increasing length for as short a time as possible. Students can sometimes achieve part of this effect by covering a line of print with a card and sliding the card down and back in one quick action while trying to retain as much of the line of print as possible.

Varying the length of the speed drill sometimes helps. If the student has been practising on articles approximately 500 words long, the instructor might set some extremely short articles, of one or two paragraphs, to be read under timed conditions.

Finally, it might be noted that some lack of reading improvement may be due to unfamiliarity with reading. For the purposes of this course it is assumed that the student has had several years' experience reading in English. But this experience might sometimes be very meagre, and so increased familiarity with reading is recommended through practice with large amounts of easy reading matter.

Of great joy to both teacher and student is the large improvement pattern. It is not unusual for students to more than double their initial reading rate. But when a large gain has been made there is often a fair amount of variation, with reading speed

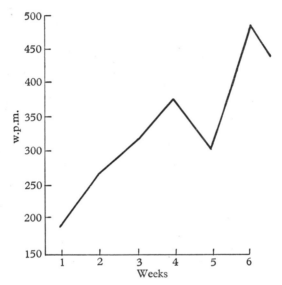

Fig. 21. Large improvement pattern.

going up and down by 100 words per minute in the course of several weeks. There are several reasons for this fairly large fluctuation in reading speed after a large gain has been made. One is the extreme shortness of the passages read. In the *Drill Book* the passages average 500 words in length. It will be noted from looking at the words-per-minute chart that with an article of 500 words, missing the reading time of one minute by just one second, and so falling within the '1 minute and

71   6-2

10 seconds' column, implies a difference of 70 words per minute in reading speed. Hence, in order to get a more accurate measure of reading speed for fast readers longer articles are needed.

Another factor in the fluctuating speed of fast readers is the newness of the habit. When a person has just learned a new skill, such as reading fast, it is often difficult for him to control it. So he will on some days have mastered it, and read very rapidly with little effort, and on other days—with seemingly a greater effort—his speed will be definitely lower. These variations can be smoothed out by practice. Students who have made very rapid gains should especially be encouraged to do large amounts of extra reading in order to establish this new and wonderful habit.

HABITS AND ENCOURAGEMENT

The teacher must work at getting the students to use their new reading habits in as many subjects as possible. Regular checking of their easy reading homework will serve as encouragement.

After six weeks of reading instruction, encouragement of the students to do better remains a continuing problem. Before each class-drill or homework exercise the teacher should encourage the pupils to do their best. This means that each pupil should be aware of his own graph, and know whether he should be emphasizing speed or comprehension. The teacher might read again the latter part of chapter 4, about high, low and balanced comprehension.

SUMMARY AND SUGGESTED LECTURE OUTLINE

1. There are many different patterns of improvement; all are normal.

2. A steady pattern is good but not too usual.

3. A sudden improvement pattern shows no gain for several weeks, then suddenly jumps up.

4. The student should avoid feeling discouraged during a period showing no improvement.

5. A plateau pattern has a levelling-off period between gains.

6. Irregular patterns are also normal. Downward trends can be caused by unfamiliarity, illness, or emotional factors.

7. Improvement may be limited by the student's poor ability (though bright students do not always make gains), or by his personality.

8. Students who do not improve can be helped by: skimming, letting comprehension drop temporarily, re-reading, tachistoscopic drill, exercises of varying length, and more easy reading.

9. A large gain is good. Fluctuation can be caused by the shortness of the exercises, or by inability to control the new skill.

10. Encourage habits of better reading. Check easy reading homework.

11. Before class-drill, encourage the students to emphasize either speed or comprehension according to the need revealed by their individual graphs (the past weeks' results).

12. Continue to set for homework speed practice, skimming practice, and easy reading.

7

STUDY TECHNIQUES AND
FACTORS IN MEMORY

Many students, and even teachers, confuse studying and reading. It is true that studying often involves reading, but if a student does nothing but reading during his study period he is not working as effectively as he might.

The study techniques described in this chapter are not different ways of reading. Reading is a part of most study techniques, but it is not and should not be the whole. Experiments have been conducted in which study techniques have been compared with ordinary reading. For example, half a class might be given a short chapter of a text-book and told to read and re-read it as many times as they could in a given period of time. The other half of the class might be told to use a study technique on the same chapter for exactly the same period of time. At the end of the time, both halves of the class should take the same test on the material in the chapter. Students who use the study technique almost always come out ahead of the students who merely read and re-read the chapter.

In the following section we shall consider one specific study technique, the 'SQ3R', which embodies many of the important learning principles found desirable in studying.

THE SQ3R STUDY TECHNIQUE

The SQ3R technique involves several steps. At first it might seem that it is less efficient than ordinary reading, but a little practice and experience will show that it is a better method of

(1) comprehending difficult material, and (2) remembering the material learnt over a period of time. Each letter of the title 'SQ3R' stands for a step. The student may wish to follow the technique as it is described, or he may wish to use only parts of it.

Survey

The S of SQ3R stands for *Survey*. When the student first approaches the material to be studied, say a chapter of a text-book, the first thing he does is to 'survey' it. This means that he lightly skims through the material, turning the pages rapidly. He may glance at the subheadings, the number of illustrations, or the figures used. He notices how long the chapter is in terms both of the actual number of pages and of the subject-matter covered. If the chapter is in a history book, he should find out whether it covers the next 10 years or the next 500 years. In terms of gestalt psychology (which we discussed in an earlier chapter), the student should get an overall view of the whole chapter. He should form a rough outline that can later be filled in by more careful reading of the chapter.

The survey should not take much time. For example, a student might spend only three minutes surveying a twenty-page chapter. He is seeking only the most general notion of what the whole chapter is about.

Questions

The letter Q in our SQ3R title stands for *Questions*. In this stage of the study technique the student is instructed to go through the chapter and make a series of questions. If the author has used subheadings it will simplify the student's task: all he will have to do is to change the subheadings into questions. If, for example, the chapter is on electricity, the first heading might be *Direct Current*. The student then forms a question such as 'What is direct current?' This question might do if the chapter is an introductory one on electricity, but in a more advanced text-book the student might have to ask a more sophisticated question such as 'How is direct current used in this process?' The questions asked should always be as intelligent as possible and related to the material in the chapter as directly as possible.

The student might ask, 'What do you mean by *ask* questions? Does it mean ask mentally, or write down on a sheet of paper?' It is best if the students write the question down. Written questions are useful for later reference. The student need not always write down the question in full: he might, for example, merely write down 'D.C.?' (See Fig. 22 for some sample questions using the SQ3R on this chapter.)

Often the student will be studying a chapter in which there are no subheadings. He must then skim through to get the main ideas and ask questions based on these. His survey should have helped him in finding the most important areas of the chapter, and skimming should help him to pick out the main ideas in order to put them down in question form.

If the questions are extracted skilfully, they should give an outline of the chapter. This outline will usually form a more detailed gestalt than the original survey did.

Another important and interesting result of making questions on a chapter is the arousing of the student's curiosity. A student who comes to the chapter with specific questions to be answered will learn more than a student who comes with some vague idea in his head, such as 'I need to know what it is all about'. Students who are curious about a subject will certainly learn more, more easily, than students who have some vague goal such as 'finishing the course' or 'getting through an examination'.

Read

The 3R part of the title SQ3R is to suggest 'R, R, R'. The first R stands for *Reading*. Reading simply means reading the material through in such a manner that the questions can be answered. Often during reading the student will find certain areas which should have a question on them, and he can stop and write down this question. Since he is already becoming familiar with the material through previously surveying it and thinking out questions, he should be reading to check his original impressions as well as to fill in the details.

Note how different the SQ3R technique is from the way in which many people study. In many cases, a student simply reads the first page, then the second page, and so on. Often the student will begin to read the chapter without knowing whether it contains two pages or two hundred pages. He will begin not knowing what subject-matter is to be covered, or whether there will be many facts or few facts. In the SQ3R method, the student has been through all the pages at least twice before beginning to read. He turns all the pages once on his original survey, and he again turns all the pages when making up his questions.

Recite

The second R of the SQ3R technique stands for *Recite*. Recitation is an old and time-honoured method of learning, but it is often overlooked by students who are working by themselves. In recitation the student attempts to tell what he has learnt. His questions can serve as interesting stimulus to each part of the recitation. There are several ways in which recitation can be done. The student might read his own questions and attempt to think out the answers; or he might read his own questions and write out an answer, or at least outline an answer, on paper. (See Fig. 22 for an example of answers.)

Sometimes several students will study together, and one student can ask questions while the other recites. Then the students change about, and the second student asks questions and the first recites.

Note that this type of recitation involves only two students, rather than three or more. The purpose of doing this with only two students is that the most important learning technique is in the recitation, not in the listening. The important part of this section of the study technique is that the student forms in his own mind and in his own words answers to the questions, each of which involves a major point of the chapter being studied. It should also be noted that he should not attempt to repeat the author's exact words. In recitation he does not memorize an answer and give it back like a memorized poem. A student should state the ideas in his own words, not the author's, and give his own illustrations and applications rather than those used in the book.

There is another advantage in reciting with another student: he may have learned certain points from the chapter which the first student has not picked up. There is also a certain amount of social stimulation in working together, which may keep the students studying longer than they would have done by themselves. Students should be careful, however, not to make studying together just a social occasion, and they should keep their minds on their subject. If another student is not available, the answers to the questions might be recited to a parent or another interested person. (Even if the person is not interested it is still a good idea to recite the answers aloud, as this makes the student form the answers in his mind.)

Speaking aloud uses various sense-organs, in particular those involved in speech and hearing. In many ways, the SQ3R study technique is a multi-sensory approach. The student uses his eyes to read and see the material written down in the author's words and in his own questions. He uses the nerves and sense-organs involved in writing out questions and outlining the material. He uses further sense-organs in speaking the material, and again he hears both himself and sometimes another student giving the material in oral form. All these

What does SQ3R *mean?*	Survey, Question, Read, Recite and Revise.
What does 'Survey' mean?	Turn all the pages in the chapter being studied, see how long it is, and get a general idea of the content.
What is meant by 'Question'?	Write down questions on each main point in the chapter (as in the column on the left here). Base the questions on the main points, which can be deduced from the subheadings or extracted by skimming.
What does 'Read' mean?	Read the chapter completely to answer the questions. Note that reading is not done first.
What is meant by 'Recite'?	Answer the questions completely, either orally to another person or in writing, putting answers in your own words (as in this column).
What does 'Revise' mean?	Some days later the material should be revised, possibly by quickly re-reading the chapter, and/or trying to answer the questions, looking up all wrong or partial answers.

Fig. 22. Sample questions and recitation (answers) using the SQ3R study technique.

various ways in which the material is handled make the method appropriate to the different types of student, such as those who prefer listening and those who prefer a visual approach.

It might also be noted that another important learning principle is being used in this technique, and that is 'activity'. In order for learning to take place, activity is often highly desirable. Sometimes straight reading tends to be a passive function in which the student merely follows the author's thinking. In the SQ3R study technique the student must examine the material carefully, first in looking for the main ideas, then in changing these main ideas into questions, and finally in answering the questions. He reads with curiosity, always trying to find something specific. His recitation period is perhaps the most active of all the stages, as here he must re-cast the material into his own language.

Revise

Thus far in following this technique the student has been through the material four different times in one way or another. By this time he is probably tired of it and going through it yet again would add to his annoyance rather than to his learning. Hence the last R of the SQ3R technique is for *Revise*. This means studying the material again later, perhaps after the passage of some days.

Psychologists have found that the period of most rapid forgetting is just after learning. This means that we all have a great tendency to forget something just after we have learnt it (see Fig. 23). But if we revise the material the forgetting does not take place so rapidly. Note in Fig. 24 that a review of the material has taken place after three days. During this revision the student re-learnt 100% of the material (it did not take him as long, this time), and following the revision the forgetting took place much more slowly. This is the reason why teachers so often force their students to revise by having tests at the end of the week or month. By thus forcing the student to revise the material some time after the initial learning, high retention over a longer period of time is secured.

In the SQ3R technique, the revision might be done in any one of several ways. The student might re-read the chapter rapidly, then glance over his questions and answer them in his

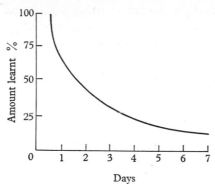

Fig. 23. A typical forgetting curve.

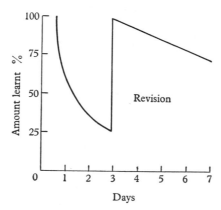

Fig. 24. Forgetting curve with revision. Note that after revision forgetting occurs (curve drops) less rapidly.

mind. If he has done a good job of writing the questions and answers, he might merely read his own questions and answers. Or he might revise with another student, the two taking turns to ask questions and to answer them. The revision should not take as long as the initial study. Having once been over the material carefully in the first four steps of the SQ3R technique, it is not necessary to spend an equal amount of time in the revision period.

As most students already know, it is important to revise material before an examination. If the examination is a major one and covers a lot of material, the revision should probably take place a day or two before the examination. Trying to cram in facts up to the very moment of walking to the door of the examination room often leads to mental fatigue and confusion. A student will usually do much better in an examination if he has learnt the material earlier, revised it within the few days preceding the examination, then had a satisfactory rest period, such as a good night's sleep, before taking the papers.

FURTHER STUDY TECHNIQUES AND FACTORS IN MEMORY

In the preceding section, we have been studying the SQ3R study technique which embodies many established principles in learning. But there are a number of other principles related to learning which should be of interest both to the student and teacher, and we shall discuss these in this section.

Activity

'Activity' is an important factor in learning. Most learning involves some type of mental activity, but because it is difficult for mental activity to be observed by the teacher some type of physical activity such as writing is often required. Students may also find it helpful in ensuring mental activity if they do some sort of physically active work.

There are many ways in which students can maintain physical activity while working. One of the simplest is to stop at frequent intervals and think about the material. Another way of ensuring some activity is to outline the study material. This

Good underlining picks out main ideas and important points

> Activity is an important factor in learning. Most tasks require at least some type of mental activity in order for them to be mastered by the student. Because it is difficult for mental activity to be seen by the teacher, often some type of physical activity such as writing is required. Students also might find it helpful to ensure mental activity if they force themselves to do some sort of physically active task.

Bad underlining has too much material underlined

> Activity is an important factor in learning. Most tasks require at least some type of mental activity in order for them to be mastered by the student. Because it is difficult for mental activity to be seen by the teacher, often some type of physical activity such as writing is required. Students also might find it helpful to ensure mental activity if they force themselves to do some sort of physically active task.

Bad underlining has the wrong parts underlined

> Activity is an important factor in learning. Most tasks require at least some type of mental activity in order for them to be mastered by the student. Because it is difficult for mental activity to be seen by the teacher, often some type of physical activity such as writing is required. Students also might find it helpful to ensure mental activity if they force themselves to do some sort of physically active task.

Fig. 25. Good and bad underlining as a study technique.

might be done by writing out an outline in a note-book, or by underlining in the text-book if it belongs to the student.

If the student uses underlining as a method of study, care should be taken to see that the underlining represents careful

Outlining	Notes

Activity important for learning
(a) Mental activity
    (1) stop and think
(b) Physical activity
    (1) outlining
    (2) underlining
    (3) note-taking
    (4) personal index
    (5) SQ3R
	Activity, both physical and mental are important for learning. Student may stop and think, outline chapter, underline book, take notes on reading, make a personal index, or use the SQ3R technique.

Practice important for learning
(a) Both physical and mental skills
(b) Mere repetition not enough
    (1) try to improve each time
(c) Space out practice
(d) Use things learnt
    (1) new vocabulary in speaking
    (2) reading skills on newspaper
	Practice is also important for learning both physical and mental skills. Student should try to improve each time; mere repetition not enough. Practice should be spaced out and use should be made of things learnt.

Note the similarity between outlining, notes and underlining (Fig. 25). All strive for main ideas. Outlining and note-taking are possibly more 'active' than underlining. Outlining gives a better visual picture (gestalt) and shows system more clearly. Outlines or notes taken on reading are most often kept in note-books, but sometimes they are kept on file cards for handy reference or study.

Fig. 26. Examples of outlining and note-taking for study.

thinking and selection of the most important parts of the material. Mere underlining of words without careful selection is not a good study technique. (See Fig. 25.)

Some students find it more helpful merely to take notes of interesting or important parts of what they read. ('An outline' implies that the student would be systematically covering all the material, while 'notes' implies that only selected items are written down.) (See Fig. 26.)

A similar and important technique is making an index by listing subjects and pages on which they appear. With his own index the student can refer to the text-book when he needs certain information.

In the SQ3R study technique, we see that activity of a mental nature is required in both the survey and the revision part, while activity of a more physical nature is required in the questions and recitation steps.

Practice

Practice is also important for learning. Perhaps it is more necessary for learning physical skills than mental skills, but it is useful for both. The student should remember that mere repetition is not enough. He must practise with diligence, that is he must try to improve each time he repeats a piece of work.

Many types of learning seem to take place better if there are spaces in the practice. Hence school courses in subjects such as reading improvement are frequently spread out over a number of weeks so that there will be practice, followed by an interval, followed by more practice, and so on. At least some of the intervals during practice should be rest periods.

Another type of practice which is not used nearly enough is the attempt to use the material learnt. For example, if the student is working on vocabulary, he should attempt to use the newly learned words in everyday conversation, even though at first he may have to force them into his speech. If he is working on reading improvement, he should practise reading skills while reading the newspaper and not just on the exercises set.

It will be noted that when using the SQ3R study technique the student goes over the material at least four times while studying; then further practice is given later in the form of revision.

System

It is easier to learn things if they are arranged in some sort of order or system. This is why school subjects are arranged in different courses, and courses divided up into units; and why books are written on specific subjects, those subjects divided into chapters, and chapters divided into sections. If the student can see things in some sort of plan or pattern, it will help him to learn. Sometimes things seem to fall together naturally. For example, a number of different types of addition problems can be grouped together; or the history of England during a certain period can be studied as one unit before going on to study the history of Germany in the same age.

Outlining is an attempt to give the subject some type of organization. Sometimes students will study by making charts or diagrams of the subject-matter, and this is an aid both to understanding it and to remembering it. Even a very loose or informal organization such as a student might make up himself is often helpful in remembering the material.

Organizing the material often adds meaning, and meaning has been found to be a great aid to memory. By organizing the material, relationships between the parts are often brought out, and the meaning of a part is enhanced by its being seen in relation to other parts.

Association

Some types of learning seem to be largely the making of an association between one fact and another fact. In learning a foreign language, for example, a student must learn how words in the foreign language correspond to words in his own language. A useful study technique in foreign languages is to write the foreign word on one side of a small card, and the corresponding native word on the back, until a pile of cards has been made. The student then takes the cards one by one, looking at the native word and trying to recall the foreign word; he checks his answer by turning the card over. Sometimes he should turn the stack over and look at the foreign word first and try to recall the native word. He may get selective practice by sorting out the cards on which he has trouble in making the association, and working on these cards more intensively.

By studying words in this manner, he is making use of an important factor in associative learning: closeness in time. He looks at the foreign word and quickly thereafter is given the native word. This shortness of time between the occurrence of the two factors being associated is a help. The immediate correction of any error is also important.

Another type of closeness useful in association is similarity in meaning or units or sounds. For example, in learning to count in Spanish, students will find it easy to learn that *uno* means 'one' because they have a similar sound. He will find that 'five' is a little harder to remember because the Spanish word is *cinco* because there is not the similarity of sound. But if he knows the French *cinq* this will establish a similarity. Emphasizing the parts of a new subject that are similar to a known subject makes it easier to learn the new subject. In associative learning, the student should make use of as many forms of closeness as possible.

Another type of association is the use of mnemonic devices. A good example is 'SQ3R' where the S stands for *Survey*, Q stands for *Questions*, etc. Another example of a mnemonic device is the physics student's old friend 'Roy G. Biv'. Each letter of this name stands for a colour of the spectrum so that the colours of the spectrum are red, orange, yellow ('Roy'), etc. In some subjects, students find it quite helpful to make up mnemonic devices in order to memorize lists of facts which otherwise have no particular system or meaning.

The so-called tricks of memory (*memoria technica*) are done by association. Using some of these tricks people can perform amazing feats of memory, such as memorizing a hundred-digit number in only a few minutes, or learning a list of twenty objects in a very short time so that they can call them off in order, or forwards or backwards, or by number, and so on. (A description of how to do one of these interesting tricks is given in Appendix 2. It is useful in that it shows the power of associative learning, and may also be useful in helping the student to memorize a list of facts at some time.) The ancient Greeks considered it important for students to learn elaborate mnemonic devices so that they could remember dates in history, or places in geography, as very few of them were able to afford books.

Use all the senses

Some students may be able to learn a thing more easily if they hear it, while other students can learn it more easily if they see it. Certain types of material are better presented in words, and others better presented in schematic diagrams. In order to take advantage of these personal differences and differences in material, it is well to try using as many different senses as possible. For example, in the SQ3R method the student sees the material in the book and again in his own written questions; he has the sensation of writing down the material in the question-and-answer form; he then both speaks and listens to the material. In this way there are many different sense-organs involved in the learning process.

Many students find that they have a strong visual memory. If they can picture a subject they can remember it much longer. In studying, it is well to pay careful attention to pictures and diagrams in the text-book. Sometimes a student's study can be greatly aided if he makes his own simple pictures or charts of the material.

Guidance and trial and error

In studying new material, it is well to give a generous amount of guidance. This means that the student should carefully follow a model. For example, in speaking a foreign language a student should hear the word repeated several times and then try to imitate what he hears. In studying history, the student should first listen to the lecture or read the text-book carefully. In this way he is being guided by the teacher or writer through the subject. After he has had guidance he should try to learn by a trial-and-error method. This means he should try to use the words the teacher has said, to answer questions on or recast the lecture or reading, in an original way (where he is more likely to make errors). In following this plan, the student has no opportunity to make a mistake at the very first stage of learning because he is being carefully guided by the teacher or writer. In the second stage, the student has an opportunity to make mistakes and is exercising his own judgement. During the trial-and-error period, he should have an adequate chance to correct his own answers by looking back at the text-book or hearing the instructor again, or seeing a corrected test paper, so that any mistakes he makes are corrected as soon as possible.

The 'guidance before trial and error' principle is seen in many school lessons where the student has a lecture or a chapter to read, followed by questions. A student can follow this principle in his own studying.

Mental attitudes

Intention is extremely important in learning. If you tell a student that you will give him a lot of money for remembering the answer to a question, he will probably remember it quite easily and for a long time. If a student has a strong desire to do well in his work, to please his parents or to keep up with or do better than his friends, he is apt to study much harder and learn more. The teacher should try to develop the strongest possible motives in the student to help him in his learning.

Meaning is another important factor in learning. If the student can find meaning and order in his subject, he will be able to assimilate it much more easily than if it is presented merely as a random series of facts. When studying, the student should try to see that what he is learning has meaning for him in his own life. He should think up his own meaning or examples to the principles that are being taught.

Emotion also plays a part in learning. If a student is emotionally disturbed he will find learning difficult. Emotional problems at home or in school can affect his work. Another important aspect of emotion is that pleasant material tends to be learnt more easily than unpleasant material. If the student can somehow associate pleasure with what he is learning, he will find that he remembers it longer than if the material has unpleasant associations for him.

Learning also takes discipline. It is often not easy to study, and the student must supply a good measure of self-discipline to sit down and concentrate. Good working habits are indispensable for learning a large amount of material. The student should discipline himself to work regularly for a certain number of hours at a certain time each day. This is one reason for the success of schools, for they supply a regular learning discipline. The student comes to class at a regular time each day and concentrates on a specific subject. He should follow the same practice in studying on his own.

Rest is also essential during learning. If a student is tired he will not learn well. If he tries to learn too much at once, with no pause for recreation or break in studying, he will also lose a good deal of his learning efficiency.

Environment

The environment or surroundings in which a student studies can have an effect on his learning. If he tries to study when there is a lot of extraneous noise, such as radios playing or children running in and out, he cannot concentrate as well as if he has a quiet room. There are other important features, such as having a comfortable place to work. This means a suitable desk and chair with the necessary equipment (paper, pencils, note-books and reference-books) near at hand.

The desk should also be well lighted. Studying in a place that has too little light, or too much (such as the glare from direct sunlight), can cause eye strain and fatigue which will force the student to stop working.

Recall

In studying, the student should keep in mind what kind of 'recall' (bringing back to memory) he is going to need for the material. 'Unaided recall' is perhaps the most difficult form. An example of a question calling for unaided recall is 'Describe life in England during the Middle Ages'.

Somewhat easier is the type of question which is known as 'recognition' or 'aided recall'. This type includes the usual 'true and false' questions, or 'multiple-choice' questions in which the student is given a choice of several answers. It is easier to study for this type of test, as the student merely has to recognize the correct answer and not recall it unaided from his memory.

Selectivity is another important factor of recall. We all know people who in telling a story include every detail to a point where they bore the listeners to death. Students, likewise, in answering questions sometimes throw in so many trivial details that they never get to the main point. In attempting to answer any examination question the student should think carefully about the answer before writing anything down. He might go so far as to outline an answer and then stop and think about the outline to make sure the main points are all covered. Sometimes students fail to demonstrate that they have learnt the material properly, because they lack selectivity. Selectivity can be learnt and with practice it can become a habit; a very good habit for the student to have.

SUMMARY AND SUGGESTED LECTURE OUTLINE

1. Studying is different from reading and includes other activities.

2. The SQ3R study technique was described. The S stands for *Survey*, which means to turn all the pages of a chapter being studied, lightly skimming, reading subheadings, and glancing at pictures to get a general idea of the length of the chapter and the scope of the material.

3. Q stands for *Question*, which means that the student should make up questions about each main point of the chapter, using subheadings of skimming to find the main ideas.

4. The first R means *Read* the chapter in order to answer the questions. Reading may show new points that need questions. Note that reading is not done first.

5. The second R means *Recite*. Answer the questions, either aloud to another student or by writing answers. Use your own words and examples.

6. The last R means *Revise*. At a later time (after several days), revise the material by fast re-reading and/or reading questions and forming answers. Revision helps to retain material longer.

7. Other study methods include activity, both mental and physical. Techniques include: stopping to think about the

reading, outlining, note-taking, underlining, and making an index.

8. Practice is important and must be done with diligence. Practice should be spaced out and should include application of what has been learnt.

9. Arranging things in a system makes it easier to learn them.

10. Much learning consists of associating one fact with another. Association is helped by closeness in time, and similarity of kind. Mnemonic devices use letters or symbols to associate facts (e.g. SQ3R).

11. Use as many senses as possible in learning, particularly the visual sense. Writing, speaking, and listening make use of other senses.

12. Proceed from guidance to trial and error. First show the student the way and guide him carefully so that he cannot make a mistake, then allow him to try it with the possibility of error and correction.

13. A good mental attitude is important for learning and includes intention, meaning, emotion, rest, and discipline.

14. A good study environment includes a quiet, well-lit room and reference-books.

15. Study for a particular type of recall, either recognition or unaided recall. Select the material for answers carefully.

8

VISION

A person with normal vision can read for at least six hours almost without stopping and without any bad effects such as headache or eye-strain. People who have visual defects cannot read for as long, and fatigue or eye-strain often begins to show after only ten or twenty minutes of reading. Frequently, the reader will not realize that the trouble is his eyes. He may think that he is just unable to read, or that he is not feeling well.

Let us discuss some common faults of vision which hinder reading.

SHORT-SIGHTEDNESS

Short-sightedness, or *myopia*, means that the person can see clearly at close range but not in the distance. A short-sighted person will not be able to see the writing on a blackboard clearly. If his degree of short-sightedness is extreme he will not be able to see the writing at all.

It is quite easy to detect short-sightedness by the wall-chart test. A normal person can see the 20/20 line standing back twenty feet from the chart on the wall. If he has slight myopia he may not be able to see the 20/20 line but he may be able to see the 20/30 line. This is still within the normal range. He is allowed to miss two letters on the line and still pass. If a student misses more than two letters on the 20/30 line he should be referred to an eye specialist for further examination. Extremely short-sighted pupils can often be noticed in class, as they hold the book very close to their eyes.

Short-sightedness can easily be corrected by glasses. Again, the student should be referred to as good an eye specialist as possible. The short-sighted student may not have to wear his glasses while reading, but he should wear them when looking at the blackboard, watching a film in the cinema, driving, or any other activity requiring seeing in the distance. Short-sightedness is caused by an eyeball that is too long, and properly fitted glasses are the only known correction.

N T O L

A E H C

Fig. 27. Wall-chart vision test (20/30 line).

LONG-SIGHTEDNESS

Long-sightedness or *hyperopia*, as the doctors call it, is a condition caused by malformation of the eyeball. The eyeball is a little too short for normal vision, hence the person must constantly strain when he is looking at something near. A long-sighted person can see objects in the distance very clearly and will easily pass the type of eye test which has letters on a chart to be read from twenty feet away. Hence, if a school uses a vision test which consists only of reading letters from a distance of twenty feet, they will never discover which students are long-sighted.

Long-sightedness causes strain in reading, because the person must make extra effort to focus on a book, which is usually held only sixteen inches away from the eyes. Young children usually have very strong eye muscles and so can focus fairly easily, even if they are long-sighted. So we see that extreme signs of visual fatigue are not likely to show in very young children. However, if even a young child spends many hours reading, and has faulty vision, he will have eye-strain. The older the student gets, the harder it is for him to keep exerting the effort to see things close at hand if he is long-sighted. Illness or fatigue can bring on strain which might not otherwise be noticed, but even when he is in the best of health a long-sighted person is using far more nervous energy to focus while reading than he should.

Long-sightedness can be detected in schoolchildren by simply using a two-diopter lens while giving the vision test. The student is first asked to read the letters on the chart. After he has read down to the normal line (20/20 if feet are used or 6–6 if metres are used), the two-diopter lens is placed in front of his eyes. If he can still read the normal lines he is long-sighted. A person with normal vision will not be able to continue to see the normal line, in other words his vision becomes slightly blurred when the two-diopter lens is placed in front of his eyes. Each eye should be tested separately, while a card is held in front of the other eye so that the student cannot use it. A two-diopter lens is quite cheap and can be obtained from any eye specialist. Do not tell the students that the way to pass the test is not to see anything.

Long-sightedness can easily be remedied by using reading-glasses. It is quite simple for any eye specialist to test and to prescribe the correct lens. Do not make the mistake of sending the student to an unqualified person, or letting him go to a shop and simply select glasses that seem to improve his vision, as this is false economy.

NORMAL EYE

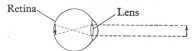

Lens changes shape with distance so that
image falls on retina at back of eyeball

LONG-SIGHTED EYE (*hyperopia*)

Eyeball is too short and lens must strain to keep image on retina

NEAR-SIGHTED EYE (*myopia*)

Eyeball is too long and lens must strain to keep image on retina

ASTIGMATIC EYE (*astigmatism*)

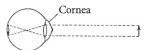

Cornea not spherical: image is never clear

Fig. 28. Common eye-defects that result in poor vision. (All these
faults can be corrected by glasses.)

ASTIGMATISM

A third fairly common eye fault is astigmatism. This is caused
by lack of roundness of the cornea. The cornea is the clear
covering of the eye through which all light must pass. In
normal eyes it is almost perfectly round (spherical). If a
person has astigmatism, the cornea has a bulge running across
it (through one axis).

97

If the person has bad astigmatism he will fail the wall-chart test, in the same way as will a short-sighted person. If a person has only slight astigmatism, as many people do, and no other defect, it usually need not be corrected. If, however, the person has either long-sight or short-sight, and he puts on glasses to have it corrected, a correction for astigmatism can be put in the glasses at the same time.

BINOCULAR CO-ORDINATION

The three faults that we have discussed above, long-sightedness, short-sightedness and astigmatism, may occur in either or both eyes. They are caused by malformation of the eye. A one-eyed person can have any of these faults. Binocular co-ordination, however, refers to the use of the two eyes working together.

When a person with normal eyes is at rest or asleep, both eyes look straight ahead in parallel lines. This means that they are at infinity. Therefore a person with normal eyes is using the minimum amount of visual energy when looking at a distant object. To look at an object near at hand, such as a book, he must converge or turn each eye inwards so that both eyeballs are aimed at the same close point. Convergence, or looking at an object near at hand, requires a little muscular energy, but for the normal person it should not involve any strain. There are, however, some people whose eyes have a tendency to aim at odd angles. An extreme form of this is cross-eyedness (*essophoria*), where one or both eyes seem to be turned in towards the nose. Another extreme form is called wall-eyedness (*exophoria*). In this condition one eye seems to be looking out towards the side.

In extreme forms of lack of binocular co-ordination, such as cross-eyedness or wall-eyedness, the student has not the ability to force his eyes to go parallel and look at an object at a distance or to get them to converge on a close object. The

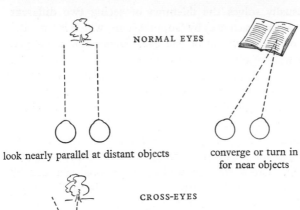

NORMAL EYES

look nearly parallel at distant objects

converge or turn in
for near objects

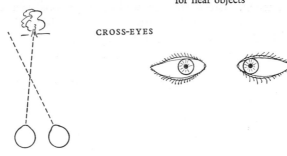

CROSS-EYES

always turn in too much

WALL-EYES

always turn out too much

Fig. 29. Binocular co-ordination.

person usually solves the dilemma of seeing two different images (one with each eye) by 'suppression', which is a mental blocking-off of the vision of one eye. Hence the cross-eyed person or wall-eyed person uses only one eye most of the time. If anything should happen to the eye that he uses, or if it is closed, he immediately sees out of the other eye. Extreme forms of lack of binocular co-ordination, such as cross-eyedness or wall-eyedness, which are visually apparent (seen by simply looking at the person) can be corrected by surgery. It is, of course, a job for a skilled surgeon, but the operation is not uncommon. Cross-eyed or wall-eyed persons can usually learn to read quite satisfactorily using only their dominant eye, but for the sake of depth perception (stereopsis) and physical appearance it is a good idea to have this condition corrected by surgery if possible.

There is a minor type of poor binocular co-ordination which it is very important for the teacher to discover. In this minor type of lack of binocular co-ordination, the student can, by straining, make both eyes go where he wants them to. This means that if you look at this student, he does not appear to be cross-eyed or wall-eyed. He has depth perception, and both eyes work together, usually at both long and short range. His eyes, however, have a *tendency* to go out (wall-eyedness) or turn in (cross-eyedness). This means that if the student is extremely tired, drunk, drugged, or asleep, his eyes will often tend to go into the position which for them is more natural, turning either out or in. When the student is healthy and awake he can control his eyes so that this condition is not apparent.

Great difficulty is caused in reading when the eyes tend to turn outwards. The student has to use extra muscular energy to keep his eyes parallel when looking at an object in the distance; but to look at a near object such as a book he must use an abnormal amount of energy, and this causes fatigue and many symptoms of eye-strain, such as red cords or irritation in the eye, sties, headaches, or a general disinclination to read or look at anything close. If the student's eyes tend to turn in, it may be even less strain for him to read than for the normal person, but he will have great difficulty in looking at distant objects such as a cinema screen or blackboard for any period of time.

Minor lacks of binocular co-ordination are difficult for the classroom teacher to detect. They can be detected through tests which use a stereoscope and special test cards.* If the school has no regular examination for binocular co-ordination, a quick and fairly simple test can be made by the teacher's examining the motor muscles in the eyes. This is not as accurate a test as those mentioned above, and it requires a little judgement and skill on the part of the teacher, but it is considerably better than nothing.

The way to administer the eye muscle test is simply to get the student to face the teacher. The teacher then tells him to look at the end of a pencil. The teacher moves the pencil in a large circle around his face so that he must look up, to the side, down, and to the other side. The circle should be close to the student's face, so that he must strain to see it, and he must not be allowed to turn his head, only his eyes. After this the pencil should be moved closer and closer to the student's nose, and he should follow the point in until he looks as though he were cross-eyed. By watching the student's eyes, the teacher can see if both eyes follow the movement of the pencil. If they do not, he should be referred to an eye specialist for further examination. An especially critical part of this test is moving the pencil in towards the student's nose. A student with normal vision can keep both eyes on the pencil until it almost touches his nose. If he can keep both eyes on the pencil until it is

* Tests for binocular co-ordination used in American schools include the Keystone Telebinocular, American Optical Company Orthorater and the Massachusetts Eye Tests.

(1) Make a circle in air around student's face with a pencil. Student follows pencil with eyes. Teacher watches eyes. If student cannot follow it, particularly at the extreme sides, he fails.

(2) From straight out, move pencil nearer and nearer to student's nose.

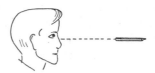

Student should be able to follow pencil to 4 inches or less.

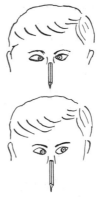

If he cannot (one or both eyes do not follow) then refer to a specialist.

This test is for minor faults in binocular co-ordination. Students with major faults, such as crossed-eyes or wall-eyes, will of course fail. Students who fail should be sent to an eye specialist for further examination.

Fig. 30. Eye-muscle test.

within four inches of his nose, he still passes. But if his eyes 'break' (this means that one eye stops following the pencil and looks out, or simply stops moving) at any distance greater than four inches from his nose, he should be referred to an eye specialist.

Correction of minor faults of binocular co-ordination is a matter of controversy. Some eye specialists will do nothing about it. Others will correct the trouble with glasses which are specially ground (prisms). This is usually a satisfactory correction. Some eye specialists recommend eye exercises for this condition. How much eye exercises help this condition is at present a matter of controversy, and the teacher had best be guided by the specialist.

TEN RULES FOR HEALTHY VISION

1. *Always have adequate light for reading*

Man's eyes were originally made for outdoor use. Good light makes it easier to see, and even cuts down eye-strain where there are minor defects of vision. Artificial light can seldom be too strong, but reading from a white page in direct sunlight may cause slight eye-strain. It may be difficult for teachers to judge the proper amount of artificial light, but as a rough guide we shall say that a 100 watt bulb between three and seven feet from the printed page, together with other bulbs to give the room general illumination, should be satisfactory.

2. *Avoid glare*

Glare can distract the student from reading and cause some eye-strain. It can be received from shiny desk tops or shiny book-pages (just as from a mirror). It is caused by having the main source of illumination (the light bulb or open window) in the wrong position. For example a study light which is directly ahead of the student may cause a glare to come directly on the desk or the printed page. The student should not read facing the window or facing the bright light bulb, but should have the light coming from the side, the top, or over his shoulder.

3. *Avoid a dark background*

Books are usually printed with a margin around the type to make it easier for the student to see the printed words. Better books have wider margins, and this contributes to greater reading ease. However, even beyond the margins of the book, there should be a light or neutral background. Light wood for desks is much better than dark wood, and light-coloured desk blotters are better than dark ones. It is better for the student to read in a room which is generally lighted than to have a light on the page and the rest of the room dark.

4. *Look at infinity to rest*

The eyes were made mostly for distant vision; this means looking at objects twenty feet or more away. Students who try to study in too small a room with no windows may get a confined feeling. This could be caused by the need for the eyes to relax and look in the distance occasionally. Students will usually be happier studying in large rooms than in small cubicles, unless the cubicles have windows. After the student has been reading or studying for a while, it is restful for him to look up at some object twenty feet or more away. Closing the eyes for a moment may also help them to return to a position of rest.

5. *Change body position*

While reading or studying, students often sit in one fixed position for long periods of time. It is relaxing to the eyes as well as the rest of the body if there can be changes in the body position. After studying for a while, the student should get up and stretch and walk around for a while. He might sit first in one position and later in another.

6. *Watch for symptoms of eye-strain*

Some of the common symptoms of eye-strain are: redness of the eye; inflamed eye-lids; headaches in the temples, the back of the head, or other parts of the head; noticeable uneasiness while doing some visual task such as reading or whilst looking at a distant object for a long time, or holding the book much nearer or farther away from the eyes than is normal.

7. *Watch for diseases of the eye*

A common disease of the eye is conjunctivitis or 'pink-eye', which often occurs in schoolchildren. One or both eyeballs turn quite red and have a feeling of irritation. A white discharge also appears in the corners of the eyes. This discharge forms a crust, which can often be seen in the morning after the eyes have been shut all night. This disease spreads rapidly among schoolchildren, usually because they touch their irritated eyes and then touch another child who in turn touches his eyes. Students with this condition should be sent to the doctor, and then told to stay at home to avoid spreading the disease. It can be fairly easily cured with drugs, but if left unattended could become serious. Sties or other forms of inflammation of the eyelids are sometimes the cause of eye strain, and in any event should be seen by a doctor. There are many other diseases of the eyes, some of which are serious and can cause blindness. At any sign of eye infection, the student should be sent to a doctor.

8. *Remove foreign objects carefully*

Children, and sometimes adults, get bits of sand, dirt or other foreign matter in the eye. If it is small, it can sometimes be removed by the student's keeping his eye closed and allowing the tears to wash the object to the corner of his eye. A larger object sometimes gets stuck, and the eyelid should be pulled back and the object removed with the aid of a matchstick covered by clean soft cotton cloth or cotton-wool. Sometimes a foreign object can be rinsed from the eye by pouring in a small amount of clean water or using an eye cup. If difficulty is encountered in getting an object out of the eye, or if the object is dangerous— such as broken glass or a fragment of metal—it should be removed by a doctor. In any event, the student should never rub the eye when something gets into it. If he gets something in his eye he should first close his eyes for a minute or two, and if this is not satisfactory, seek help in the removal of the object.

Students should also be warned against looking at extremely bright things, such as a welding torch or the sun, without specially made dark glasses. Looking at bright objects can cause damage to eyes.

9. *Use glasses if needed*

If the student is short-sighted or long-sighted, and needs glasses, it is foolish not to use them. Struggling along with imperfect vision only uses energy which could otherwise be put to better use. It also frequently causes a strong disinclination to study or read, and this can sometimes be disastrous.

If glasses are not needed, they will not help. Some students think that magic accrues from putting on glasses, but if they have normal eyes glasses will do nothing. The wearing of uncorrected dark glasses will not relieve eye-strain if corrective glasses are needed.

Students are usually unaware that they need glasses. Eye tests should be given to every student and teacher.

10. *Watch eye balance*

It is easy for a student to think that his eyes are satisfactory if he can see accurately both at distance and near at hand. But minor difficulties in binocular co-ordination frequently go undetected and cause symptoms of eye-strain.

SUMMARY AND SUGGESTED
LECTURE OUTLINE

1. A person with normal vision can read for six hours without strain.

2. A short-sighted person cannot see well in the distance, sometimes even at reading distance, because his eyeball is too long. He could not read Fig. 27 at twenty feet.

3. A long-sighted person can see normally in the distance but must strain to see near at hand because his eyeball is too short.

4. Astigmatism is a common fault caused by a lack of roundness in the cornea (front clear part of eye). It results in some blurring at a distance and close at hand.

5. Good binocular co-ordination is necessary for close and distant vision. Even minor tendencies towards cross-eyedness or wall-eyedness can cause eye-strain.

6. Tests for the above conditions include the letter-chart on the wall to detect short-sightedness and astigmatism, the lens test to detect long-sightedness, and the eye-muscle test to detect faults in binocular co-ordination.

7. The above faults can be corrected by glasses. Any student failing the teacher's eye tests should be sent to an eye specialist for further testing.

8. The ten rules for healthy vision are:
   (1) Always have adequate light for reading.
   (2) Avoid glare.
   (3) Avoid a dark background.
   (4) Look at infinity to rest.
   (5) Change body position.
   (6) Watch for symptoms of eye-strain.
   (7) Watch for diseases of the eye.
   (8) Remove foreign objects carefully.
   (9) Use glasses if needed.
   (10) Watch eye balance.

9

PHONICS

Good readers should know something of the relationship between the letters that they read and the speech sound that they represent. This relationship is called phonics. Sometimes an unfamiliar printed word will become familiar when spoken; and learning completely new words is often aided by pronouncing the word as well as seeing it.

Most writing, and this certainly includes English, is based on speech or oral communication. The fundamental way of transmitting an idea from one person's mind to another person's mind is through the medium of spoken language. Writing is an attempt to put spoken language down on paper. To do this we use a set of symbols called letters, which are collectively known as the alphabet. By definition, an alphabet is a group of symbols which stand for speech sounds.

There is another method of communicating written ideas which is used in other cultures. The Chinese, for example, use a system of characters which stand directly for a concept or idea. If a Chinese wishes to write *house*, for example, he will put down a single character which stands for the idea of 'a house'. The character does not stand for a particular speech sound, so that people in north China, who cannot talk to people in south China because their speech is different, can read the writing of the southern Chinese (and sometimes even the Japanese), because they use the same characters. Primitive societies also have this kind of picture-writing, or a less developed set of symbols which work in essentially the same way.

In completely phonetic writing we have a symbol to represent each speech sound. Perhaps originally English was like this, and was a '100% phonetic' language. But after centuries of constant change and evolution, and language influences from many different sources, English is no longer 100% phonetic. Some letters used in writing English have a dozen or so sounds. How phonetic is the English language? Experts disagree, because languages are very complex and there are different ways of classifying each sound. The question is made more complicated by the wide variety of dialects used in English. However, most experts would agree that English is more than 50% phonetic, and those who believe in phonics sometimes claim that it is as high as 87% phonetic. Occasionally, by stretching the imagination and using a large number of rules, someone will claim that English is 90% or more phonetic; but certainly no ordinary reader would bother to learn such a large number of phonetic principles.

Is phonics then worth teaching? Yes, it is, because if we can have a set of rules which works more than 50% of the time, and is not too much trouble to learn, it is probably well worth knowing in a subject of such importance and such frequent use as reading skill. Perhaps children learning to read should be taught the major phonic rules in the first few years of instruction. But this is often not done, and many adults, including teachers, have a very weak knowledge of phonics. Phonics is still of use to adults because even they, if they are doing any volume of reading at all, will come across new words that they have never seen before. It is helpful if they know something about the pronunciation of these words. A knowledge of phonics will also sometimes help spelling, but there are so many exceptions or possible choices that here phonics should be considered no more than a partial guide.

In spoken English there are about 42 different speech sounds or 'phonemes'. The experts differ over the exact number. Some say 39, some say 44; but it is not very important, for there is general agreement on the main speech sounds, the disagreement over the total is partly due to combinations and fine distinctions which do not trouble the ordinary reader. To write these 42 speech sounds, we have an alphabet of only 26 letters. Worse than that, at least 3 letters in the alphabet are no good at all, as they do not represent a speech sound. For example the letter *c* sometimes sounds like an *s* (in *city*) and sometimes like a *k* (in *cat*), but there is no sound peculiar to the letter *c*. The other two worthless letters are *x* and *q*; *x* usually makes a *ks* sound as in *box* and *q* is usually used with *u* and makes the *kw* sound as in *queen*.

However, let us study the useful letters that we have.

Language experts have broken English letters into two rough categories: vowels and consonants. There is disagreement at times (as over almost everything else in language) over what is a vowel sound and what is not. Still, we shall find a rough breakdown useful. What is the difference between a vowel and a consonant? It is difficult to say, but here are some of the characteristics of vowels. A vowel always uses the vocal cords: for example, *a* as in *ate* or *e* as in *me* cannot be made without using the vocal cords. A consonant may or may not use the vocal cords. The sounds made by *f* as in *fit* or *t* as in *top* do not use the vocal cords. Another distinction is that a vowel is a relatively open and flowing sound which can be elongated as much as desired. This does not always apply to consonants; for example, the *t* sound must be made short and quick. Also the passage of air through the speaker's mouth is often twisted and contorted in making consonants, whereas the mouth is relatively open in vowel sounds. Note the use of the lips in blocking the air in making the *b* sound as in *boy*. Or note the whistling of air through the teeth in making the *f* sound. Now contrast this with the sound made by *i* in the phrase *I am* or constrast it with the sound made by the vowel *a* as in *a boy*.

Another important difference between vowels and consonants is that a vowel must be present in every English word—in fact, every English syllable. This is the definition of a syllable: a separate vowel sound. We can have a one-syllable word; in fact, we can have a one-letter syllable, and so a one-vowel word. '*I*', for example, is a word. '*A*' is a word, but there is no word which is *t* or *f* or *m*. Hence, vowels can stand alone, but consonants cannot. Consonants must always lean on a vowel (be used in combination with a vowel) when used in speaking English.

CONSONANTS

A glance at Table 4 shows the consonant sounds which are represented by single letters. Consonants are much easier to work with than vowels, because most of them have only one sound, whereas vowels have a number of different sounds. However, there are two consonants which have several sounds besides the letter *c* which we have already discussed. These are the letters *g* and *s*. *G* sometimes makes its own sound, as in *good*, but it also makes a *j* sound, as in *general*. The rule is that *g* makes its own sound before *a*, *o* and *u*, as in *good*, *gad*, and *gut*. It makes its *j* sound before the vowels *i*, *e* and *y*. There are exceptions to this rule, of course, but it frequently applies. Incidentally, *c* breaks down into the same classification: making the *s* sound before *i*, *e* and *y*, and the *k* sound before *a*, *o* and *u*. The other consonant which makes two sounds is *s*. *S* usually makes its own sound at the beginning of a word or syllable but sometimes at the end of a word or syllable it makes a *z* sound, as in *is* or *has*.

b as in *boy*	*n* as in *none*
d as in *dog*	*p* as in *pot*
f as in *fish*	*r* as in *ring*
g as in *girl*	*s* as in *sister*
h as in *hat*	*t* as in *toy*
j as in *jacket*	*v* as in *vary*
k as in *kick*	*w* as in *wife*
l as in *lamp*	*y* as in *yellow*
m as in *mother*	*z* as in *zero*

Note: *c* has no sound of its own. Before *i, e* or *y* it sounds like an *s* (as in *city*), and before *a, o* or *u* it sounds like a *k* (as in *cat*).

x usually only makes a *ks* sound (as in *box*).

q usually only appears with a *u* (*qu*) and together they make a *kw* sound (as in *queen*).

s sometimes makes the *z* sound at the end of a word (such as *has*).

g usually makes a *j* sound before *i, e* or *y* (as in *gem*).

Table 4. Consonant sounds represented by single letters.

DIGRAPHS

Some consonant sounds are represented by a combination of two letters. The most common of these are the combinations *sh* as in *shoe*, *ch* as in *chair*, *wh* as in *wheel*, *th* as in *the*. Note that a digraph is a separate speech sound. The *sh* sound as in *shoe* does not sound like a blend between an *s* sound and an *h* sound; it is completely separate and really should have its own letter, but unfortunately (our written language being imperfect) it does not.

Just to make things more difficult, one digraph, *th*, has two sounds, which are called 'voiced' and 'voiceless' because the vocal cords are used in making the first but not the second. The two *th* sounds might be contrasted in the common words *this* (voiced) and *thing* (voiceless). Note that the mouth is held in the same position to make both sounds: the only difference between the two is in the use of the vocal cords. Unfortunately, there is no rule to tell us when we should use a voiced, and when a voiceless, *th* sound.

There are two other digraphs of minor importance worth a brief mention. These are *ph* which makes the *f* sound as in *phone*, and *ng* which makes the sound found in *sing* (which is different from an *n* and *g* blend).

These consonant combinations make their own unique sound (*phoneme*), as a single letter does.

> *ch* as in *church*
> *sh* as in *shot*
> *wh* as in *white*
> *th* (voiced) as in *their*
> *th* (voiceless) as in *thing*

Two other digraphs that might be included in this group are *ng* as in *ring* and *ph* as in *phone*.

Table 5. Consonant digraphs.

We have not discussed *blends* such as *bl* at the beginning of the word *black* or *gr* at the beginning of the word *grass*, because these do not present any particular problem to the reader as digraphs do. If the reader knows the sound of *b* as a single consonant and that of *l* as a single consonant, he can put them together to form the sound *bl*.

SHORT VOWELS

Vowels are unfortunately much more complex than consonants. Each of them has several major sounds, and many of them have a number of sounds. If the reader wishes to see the real complexity of pronouncing vowels, he may take a look at the beginning of any unabridged dictionary, which will give a dozen or more sounds for the letter *a* and nearly as many for most other vowels. We are going to simplify this considerably, because it is not necessary for good reading to know the many fine distinctions in vowel sounds. Vowel sounds also contribute more than consonants to the variations in spoken language which are known as accents or dialects.

To simplify things we will say that there are two major kinds of vowel sounds. The commoner class contains the so-called 'short' sounds. These sounds are seen in the words *at*, *end*, *is*, *hot*, *cup*. If a student has no other knowledge of phonic rules and nothing else to go by, he is better off using the short sound, in attempting to read a new word, than any of the other vowel sounds, as statistically these occur most frequently.

LONG VOWELS

The other major class of vowels contains the so-called 'long' sounds, as in the following words: *ate*, *me*, *tiny*, *go*, *rule*.

A problem immediately arises for the reader in encountering a strange word: which vowel sound should he use? There are three simple rules which will guide him in many instances:

1. *The syllable-ending rule* states that if a syllable ends in a consonant the vowel sound is short, and if the syllable ends in a vowel the vowel sound is long. Note that the word *no* ends in a vowel, and hence the vowel *o* has its long sound. If, however, we end the syllable with a consonant as in the word *not*, the vowel immediately changes to its short sound.

2. *The final 'e' rule* is one way of showing that a vowel is long although the syllable ends in a consonant. For example, in writing the word *note* we need to show that the vowel sound of *o* is the long sound. This is done by putting an *e* immediately after the consonant. Hence the final *e* rule states that an *e* at the end of a word (or sometimes the end of a syllable) makes the preceding vowel long. An *e* at the end of a word is usually not itself sounded. If we wish to make the long *e* sound at the end of a word, we usually use the letter *y* as in *funny*.

3. *The double-vowel rule* gives us yet another way of showing the long vowel sound when the syllable ends in a consonant. This rule states that when two vowels stand together, the first vowel is long and the second vowel is silent. There are a number of exceptions to this rule, but for the beginning reader

it is worth teaching. The double-vowel rule applies only to three vowels with any degree of frequency. The long *e* sound is made by the combination *ea* and *ee* as in the words *eat* and *seem*. The long *a* sound is made by the combination *ai* and *ay* (*y* is sometimes a vowel) as seen in the words *fail* and *stay*. The long *o* sound is made by the combinations *oa* and *ow* as is seen in the words *coat* and *own*.

Short vowel sounds are usually made when the syllable ends in a consonant	short *a* as in *at*
	short *e* as in *end*
	short *i* as in *in*
	short *o* as in *off*
	short *u* as in *up*
Long vowel sounds are usually made when the syllable ends in a vowel	long *a* as in *baby*
	long *e* as in *we*
	long *i* as in *tiny*
	long *o* as in *go*
	long *u* as in *duty*
Long vowel sounds are also made if an *e* follows the syllable. Note that an *e* at the end of a word is usually silent	long *a* as in *made*
	long *e* as in *here*
	long *i* as in *fine*
	long *o* as in *home*
	long *u* as in *use*
Long vowel sounds are also made by certain letter combinations	long *e* as in *ea* (*eat*)
	ee (*seem*)
	long *a* as in *ai* (*fail*)
	ay (*day*)
	long *o* as in *oa* (*coat*)
	ow (*show*)

Table 6. Long and short vowel sounds.

SCHWA

Unfortunately, the vowels have other sounds besides their long and short ones. One of the most confusing sounds made by vowels is the so-called 'general unaccented' vowel sound or 'schwa'. This sound is usually made by one of the three letters *a, e* or *o* as seen in *about, happen, other*. The *a, e* and *o* all make the same sound when they are used as a schwa. There seems to be no good way of determining just when a vowel makes this schwa

d; but it only happens when the vowel is unaccented. The
reader should at least be aware of this schwa problem, because the
schwa sound occurs frequently and a reader who did not know
about it might think that phonic rules are even more misleading
than is the case.

VOWEL PLUS 'R'

Another set of vowel sounds occur when the vowels are
followed by the letter *r*. First of all, we see that the combinations *er*, *ir* and *ur* all make the same sound, as in *her*, *girl*,
church. This should be fairly easy to remember and teach.

The combination *ar* unfortunately has two sounds. The most
common is the *ar* sound heard in *far*; but sometimes *ar* makes
the *air* sound, as in *vary* or *Mary*. The combination *or*
frequently makes the sound heard in the word *or* or *more*.

BROAD 'O' SOUND

We shall not go on and catalogue vowel sounds indefinitely;
but there is at least one other important sound, the broad *o*
sound which is written in several different ways. It is written
al as in *all*, or *aw* as in *saw*, or *au* as in *haul*. The *al*, *aw*, *au*
combinations can simply be memorized as giving the broad *o*
sound.

DIPHTHONGS

There are several vowel combinations which give a sort of
double vowel sound. A diphthong is the sound made by sliding
from one vowel sound to another. This can be seen in the *oi*
sound in *oil*.

There are two common vowel diphthongs. First there is the
oi sound in *oil*, which is also written *oy* as in *boy*.

The other common vowel diphthong is the *ou* sound in *out*.
It is written *ou* in *out* or *our*, and it is written *ow* in such words
as *how* and *down*. Unfortunately, *ow* is also used by the
double-vowel rule to make the long *o* sound in such words as
own. In these instances the letter *w* acts like a vowel.

Language experts say that each vowel sound such as the long *i* sound in I, is really a diphthong, but it is better to classify it as a long vowel sound for the sake of simplicity.

DOUBLE 'O' AND EXCEPTIONS

The preceding rules will cover most uses of vowels, but there are one or two more worth mentioning. When two *o*'s are seen together, they have either a long or short sound, as in the words *fool* or *good*.

There are, of course, many exceptions to this rule, but only one occurs with enough frequency to be worth mentioning. That is the short *e* sound of *ea* as is seen in such words as *heavy* and *head*. By the double-vowel rule, we would expect *ea* to make a long *e* sound as in *easy*, but it does not always do this. There are some exceptions, such as *head*, *heavy* and *ready*, in which *ea* makes the short *e* sound.

THE LETTER 'Y'

The letter *y* deserves special mention in that it is sometimes a vowel and sometimes a consonant. At the beginning of a word *y* is usually a consonant, as in such words as *yes* and *yet*. But at the end of a word or in the middle, *y* usually makes one of two vowel sounds. If it is at the end of a short word or a syllable in the middle of a word, it usually has a long *i* sound (as in *my*, *why* or *cyclone*). Note that in the short words there are no other vowels present. If *y* is the only vowel in a word, it is usually at the end and has the long *i* sound.

If *y* is at the end of a longer word (two or more syllables), it usually has the long *e* sound as in *funny*.

CONCLUSION

These are probably more than enough phonic rules for the average reader; but it is hoped that they will help both the teacher and the student in understanding the phonetic nature

Schwa sound (unaccented vowel sound)	is made by: *a* in *ago* *e* in *happen* *o* in *other*
Vowel plus 'r'	is made by the letter *r* following a vowel, modifying the sound as follows: (1) *ir*, *er* and *ur* all have the same sound *sir* *her* *fur* (2) *or* always makes the sound in *for* (3) *ar* makes two sounds: *ar* sound (*far*) *air* sound (*vary*)
Broad 'o' sound	is made by: *au* (*autumn*) *aw* (*awful*) *al* (*all*) *o* (*off*)
Diphthongs (double vowel sounds)	are made by: *ou* (*out*)　⎫ *ow* (*how*)　⎬ *ow* sound *oi* (*boil*)　⎫ *oy* (*boy*)　⎬ *oi* sound
Double 'o'	two *o*'s make two sounds: long *oo* (*food*) short *oo* (*look*)
'y'	makes a long *i* sound at the end of a short word and a long *e* sound at the end of a long word. It is a consonant at the beginning of a word. long *i* (*my*) long *e* (*funny*) consonant (*yes*)

Table 7. Other vowel sounds.

of the English language. Phonics are useful in helping children
to pronounce strange words which they have never seen before.
If a student is able to pronounce a word he will often recognize
it by its sound when he sees it in writing for the first time, as
the spoken word may be in his listening vocabulary but not his

reading vocabulary. It will also help the reader, if he wishes to discuss with someone a word which is new to him, to be able to pronounce it correctly. There is no substitute for the dictionary in determining accurate pronunciation, but these phonic rules will help the reader in pronouncing words when dictionaries are not available or when he has no time to look up the pronunciation of a word.

SUMMARY AND SUGGESTED LECTURE OUTLINE

1. Written English uses letters which stand as speech sounds. Translating these symbols into sound is called 'phonics'. English phonic rules work between 50 and 87% of the time, varying according to the complexity of the set of rules used.

2. English has 42 speech sounds (phonemes) and only 26 letters. Three letters, *c*, *x* and *q*, have no sound peculiar to them.

3. Vowels are open sounds (air passes through the mouth easily) which always use the vocal cords. Every syllable must have one vowel sound. Vowels all have several sounds, and a vowel sound may stand alone.

4. Consonants often block or twist sound (air is blocked by the teeth or the lips, or sent out through the nose). The vocal cords may not be used. Consonants cannot be used without a vowel. Consonants usually have only one sound (see Table 4, p. 112).

5. Digraphs are separate speech sounds that are written by two letters (*sh*, etc.). They are not blends (see Table 5, p. 113).

6. Short vowel sounds are the most common. Long vowel sounds are the next most common, and are indicated by the syllable end rule, the final *e* rule, or the double-vowel rule (see Table 6, p. 115).

7. Other vowel sounds are the schwa, vowel plus *r*, broad *o*, diphthongs, and double *o* (see Table 7, p. 118).

8. The letter *y* makes a consonant *y* sound at the beginning of a word (*yes*); a long *i* sound at the end of a short word (*my*) or in the middle of a word (*cyclone*); or a long *e* sound at the end of a word with two or more syllables (*funny*) (see Table 7, p. 118).

10

VOCABULARY AND CONTINUED READING PROGRESS

Although we have covered a number of aspects of reading, most of this course has been devoted to reading speed and comprehension. While these are undoubtedly the two major skills associated with reading, many other factors bear on the reading process, and we shall discuss them in this concluding chapter.

VOCABULARY DEVELOPMENT

The number of words that a student knows decides the difficulty of the material which he can read. At the lower extreme, if the student only knows several dozen words he can probably only read simple stories or messages. As his education continues and his knowledge of words increases, he will be able to read increasingly difficult subject-matter. Vocabulary is, of course, only one factor in the difficulty of reading matter. Some of the others are complexities of grammar, sentence structure, and subject (difficulty of ideas).

Few people who have not studied reading realize that approximately half of all written English material is composed of the 300 commonest words. You would find that they made up half of the words in this book. Certain words, then, have a very high occurrence and are used over and over again.

It has been found possible to communicate fairly complex ideas with a relatively small vocabulary. For example, a system known as Basic English has been developed which is composed of just 850 different words. Whole books on many topics have been written using only the Basic English vocabulary. But this vocabulary really gives more than 850 words, because some of the words which it contains have several meanings or several variant forms (as with *look*, *looks*, *looked*).

Educators have studied the way children, and students who are learning a new language, master vocabulary. They find that there is a steady growth in the size of the vocabulary with each year of study; but there is wide disagreement on exactly how many words children or adults know. The results of early studies suggested that children in the first grade in American schools know the meaning of 2500 words; while the results of more recent studies suggest that first-grade children know the meaning of about 17,000 words. Part of the difference is accounted for by the way in which the surveys on vocabulary were made. But even the most conservative study shows that in the first years of a primary school children learn about 1000 words a year, and this number gradually increases until in the junior secondary school they are learning the meanings of about 3000 words a year.

How many words adults know is equally a matter of controversy. Some studies suggest that children leaving secondary schools in America know an average of 47,000 words, while university students know about 58,000 words. One extremely high estimate for university graduates in the teaching profession is 250,000 words. It is not our purpose to enter into the controversy about how many words different people know, but merely to say that educated people do know the meaning of literally thousands of words. If students are to become efficient readers, they must have a large reading vocabulary. It is our purpose to discuss some of the ways in which a reading vocabulary can be increased.

The most natural and easy way of increasing vocabulary is simply through meeting words in use. If a child's teacher has a good vocabulary and uses words clearly, the child will learn them. If a student has wide reading experience and frequently encounters new words, he will learn them. If a pupil is placed in situations which call for the use of new words, such as writing compositions, or debating, or expressing himself in the classroom, this will also help him to learn new words.

LEVELS OF DIFFICULTY IN READING VOCABULARY

The teacher must be cautious in helping students to select books so that they do not embark on reading which contains too many new words. An overdose of strange words will often make a reader give up. It is best for a student to read books in which only a few new words are introduced. In other words, he should know most of the words in the book he is reading.

Level	Unknown words
Basic level (easy reading: student can read by himself for pleasure)	Fewer than 1 out of 20
Instruction level (work and study level: some help from teacher needed)	About 1 out of 20
Frustration level (too many new words: student quickly tires, gives up reading)	2 or more out of 20

Table 8. Three levels of reading difficulty based on unknown words.

An easy way of judging vocabulary difficulty for a student is to make him read a passage from the book aloud. If he makes less than one mistake in every 20 words, he can read the book for pleasure. If he makes about one mistake in every 20 words, it is a good book for 'instruction' (this means that he reads the book with some help from the teacher or from his classmates). If he makes more than one mistake in every 20 words the book is at his 'frustration level', and he will quickly tire or become bored with it unless his motive in reading it is extremely strong. So strong a motive cannot usually be consistently maintained. So the teacher might watch the 'one out of 20 rule' in selecting books for students; if the student is expected to sit by himself and read a book for pleasure over a long period of time, the ratio of new words to familiar words must be *less* than one out of 20. (See Table 8.)

Fortunately for teachers, a fair number of books have been graded according to difficulty of vocabulary. School librarians, publishers, school authorities and reading specialists frequently have lists of books for children which are graded according to vocabulary difficulty. The very easiest books for beginning reading often contain only a few dozen words. There are a fair number of books available with a vocabulary of several hundred words. There are books available for those learning English as a second language which are graded at the 500, 1000, 2000, 3000, 4000, and 5000 word levels. Beyond this, there are books which are simplified and made easier than those for full adult reading. Once books reach the 2000-word level, almost anything can be said and any subject described if a few extra technical words are allowed. The purpose of increasing a reading or speaking vocabulary beyond 2000 words is to add richness, colour, and subtlety to language, as well as to permit discussions of complex subjects. (See also Appendix 1.)

SPECIFIC TECHNIQUES OF TEACHING VOCABULARY

In the preceding section we have stated that a child's vocabulary grows naturally through years of experience. There are, however, a number of special techniques for increasing one's vocabulary which are worth mentioning.

The teaching of prefixes, suffixes and roots is a fast way of increasing the vocabulary once a student knows several thousand basic words. Just as there are several hundred words which are used over and over again very frequently, so there are certain prefixes which are used over and over again. In fact, if we take the 15 commonest prefixes we shall find that they account for over 80% of the prefixes used in a 20,000 word vocabulary. (A quarter of the words in a 20,000 word vocabulary have prefixes.) These 15 prefixes can be seen in Table 9. Learning the meaning of these prefixes will help the student to understand the meaning of many words. The teacher might help the class to remember them by using a number of examples of each prefix (which can be found in any dictionary).

ab (*from*)	dis (*apart*)	pre (*before*)
ad (*to*)	en (*in*)	pro (*in front of*)
be (*by*)	ex (*out*)	re (*back* or *again*)
com (*with*)	in (*into*)	sub (*under*)
de (*from*)	in (*not*)	un (*not*)

Table 9. The 15 commonest prefixes.

A knowledge of certain common roots will also contribute to understanding many words. A list of common word-roots can be seen in James I. Brown's list of 14 master words (see Table 10).

The teaching of suffixes can also help, but it is a good deal more complicated than the teaching of prefixes and roots.

The teaching of word families is a rapid way of increasing vocabulary. For example, if you are studying the root word *scope* which means 'view', it might be illustrated by the words *microscope*, *telescope*, etc.

There are a number of teachers' books and work-books on the development of vocabulary. These books frequently teach words by families, roots, prefixes and suffixes. They also teach synonyms, antonyms and various classes of words (a classification of words can be found in some grammar books).

An easy way of increasing vocabulary while reading is by mental underlining. By this simple procedure the student merely stops and carefully re-reads a new word when he comes across it in his reading. He tries to make out the meaning of

	Words	Prefix	Root
1.	Precept	pre- (*before*)	capere (*take, seize*)
2.	Detain	de- (*away, from*)	tenere (*hold, have*)
3.	Intermittent	inter- (*between*)	mittere (*send*)
4.	Offer	ob- (*against*)	ferre (*bear, carry*)
5.	Insist	in- (*into*)	stare (*stand*)
6.	Monograph	mono- (*alone, one*)	graphein (*write*)
7.	Epilogue	epi- (*upon*)	legein (*say, study*)
8.	Aspect	ad- (*to, towards*)	spicere (*see*)
9.	Uncomplicated	un- (*not*) com- (*together with*)	plicare (*fold*)
10.	Nonextended	non- (*not*) ex- (*out of*)	tendere (*stretch*)
11.	Reproduction	re- (*back, again*) pro- (*forward*)	ducere (*lead*)
12.	Indisposed	in- (*not*) dis- (*apart from*)	ponere (*put, place*)
13.	Oversufficient	over- (*above*) sub- (*under*)	facere (*make, do*)
14.	Mistranscribe	mis- (*wrong*) trans- (*across, beyond*)	scribere (*write*)

Table 10. Brown's 14 'master words' with common prefixes and roots for vocabulary study. (From James Brown, *Efficient Reading*. D. C. Heath, Boston.)

the word by the way it is used in the sentence. He then goes on with his reading. The trouble with many students is that they do not pay attention to new words when they come across them in reading. They simply skip over them, and hence do not learn them. Mental underlining is a system for making a student aware of a new word so that he has a chance to learn it. If he comes across the same new word in several different contexts, and pays careful attention to it each time, he will probably learn the meaning as accurately and surely as by looking up the word in a dictionary. (See Table 11.)

The dictionary of course is a basic tool in building up a vocabulary. A student should usually have a dictionary handy while working. However, if he has the habit of stopping to look up a new word every time he comes across it, it may slow down his reading to such a point that comprehension and pleasure are lost. It is far better for the student to read without looking up strange words than for him to stop reading altogether. Dictionary definitions sometimes help the student to gain a better understanding of the new word, but at other times he can gain the best understanding of the new word by studying its use in a sentence.

1st occurrence:	George was a *huge* man. He was 7 feet tall
2nd occurrence:	The *huge* fire burned down 20 homes
3rd occurrence:	The appeal was *hugely* successful. Enough money was raised to keep the project going for more than three years

If the student mentally underlines (pays special attention to) the new word *huge* each time he comes across it in these three occurrences, he knows its meaning well without the use of a dictionary.

Table 11. Examples of understanding a new word
through mental underlining.

IMPROVING ALL LANGUAGE SKILLS

Everything we do with language improves our comprehension of what we read. Practice in writing improves reading comprehension because in writing we must try to use words accurately and to understand the problems of expression. We learn the use of language from both talking and listening to others. The written language that we read is, after all, just a form of the spoken language; and any improvement in spoken language will help us with written language too. There are numerous types of experience in spoken language to be gained at school (such as acting, lectures, debates, and classroom discussion) all of which contribute towards skill in the use of language.

The experiences of everyday life will also contribute towards reading development and vocabulary development. If the student has seen a real elephant, there is much more meaning attached to the word *elephant* for him than for a student who has merely received a verbal description of the concept 'elephant'. Similarly, visual experiences 'once removed', such as looking at motion pictures or paintings contribute towards understanding in reading. So to some extent all the experience of life contributes towards the understanding of written matter. If a student is mad or sad or glad, if he becomes ill or fatigued or lavishly praised, it is all experience. At a later time when the student reads about someone else having a similar experience it will have much more meaning for him.

VARIETY IN READING

Nearly all the world's knowledge is written down in books, but not all languages have an equally rich amount of written knowledge. Unfortunately some languages are not highly developed and do not have a large literature. But, in other languages, such as English, virtually all of man's accumulated knowledge is available to the reader. A student who is learning to read should continually sample writing in many fields. He should read books or articles on philosophy or politics or history. But he should not limit his reading to learned subjects; he should also read about sport and adventure and strange places. His life would be enriched by reading in novels about the emotional experiences of others and the solutions others have found to life's problems.

Not all books, even on learned topics such as philosophy, are difficult to read. Books vary almost as much in difficulty as they do in subject—from those which are very easy to read and meant for children (or adults who are just learning a language) to those which are so difficult they are meant only for university graduates who have specialized in a certain field.

Students should have experience in reading for work as well as for pleasure. Most jobs which educated people are expected to fill have some reading connected with them. There are instructions and directions and trade journals and letters which must be read as part of many jobs. Students should know how to accomplish this professional reading efficiently without wasting time and without falling into errors of understanding. But the student should also have experience of reading for pleasure, where he can be lifted out of his sometimes not too pleasant surroundings into different worlds for an hour or two of recreation so that he may return refreshed, relaxed and sometimes with more insight.

ENCOURAGEMENT OF READING

Teachers can do a lot towards helping students to learn to read. One of the easiest and finest things that they can do is to acquaint them with the world of literature through discussions and talk. The teacher might take an interesting book, read several pages to the entire class, make a few comments on the nature of the book, and then set the book aside and allow some students to read it. If the teacher introduced two or three books a day in this manner, by the end of a school term the students would have at least heard of a number of different books and the teacher might be pleasantly surprised at the number of students who had actually picked up some of the books and read them.

Some schools have book clubs which meet for the students to exchange ideas on books. The book club sometimes actually exchanges books or helps to run, and acquire new books for, the school library. In many schools there are classroom libraries where 50 or more books are kept in the classroom for the students to read either in school when they have finished their work or at home. A class book club might help to acquire and run a classroom library with the assistance of the teacher.

The teacher can also perform a valuable function in helping to select books according to their interest and difficulty. It is a sad thing to see an eager student try to read a book which is too difficult for him and become frustrated and put the book down with his enjoyment of reading spoiled. Unfortunately some students who have had several such frustrating experiences decide that books are not for them. If, however, the teacher were aware of the student's reading ability he or she might give the student a taste for reading by first choosing for him the easier books from the class or school library. The teacher might be guided in the selection of his books for this pupil by hearing him read a page or two aloud and paying attention to the 'one out of 20' rule. After the student has read a number of books on an easy level, the teacher might then give him a slightly harder book.

Perhaps one of the most important habits to establish in children is that of reading. If the student once acquires a habit of reading for pleasure, interest and education, he quite possibly will continue it throughout his life. If on the other hand the student goes through school reading only what he absolutely must, in order to pass an examination, he will probably think of reading as nothing but 'school work' and never read on his own. Teachers should attempt to establish good reading habits in every way they can, through book clubs, classroom libraries, prizes for book reviews, free time for reading given during class and frequent mention in class of good books. Look again at Fig. 1 (p. 3).

Most school systems have book lists which are available for teachers to use with their classes. Book lists of good reading for children can be found in the public libraries or obtained from school inspectors or supervisors. Table 12 shows a list of fields in which secondary-school pupils in America like to read. Any teacher might make a similar list by simply asking his pupils, or giving them different varieties of reading and seeing which they prefer. Lists like the one found in Table 12 can then be used in selecting books for the school or classroom library.

Boys	Girls
Adventure (outdoor, war)	Adventure (not grim)
Outdoor games	Humour
School life	Animals
Mystery	Love
Humour	Family life
Stories about men (including biographies)	Stories about men and women (including biographies of women)
Science (how to make things)	Domestic arts (how to cook, etc.)

Table 12. Reading interests of American secondary-school students (grades 7–12).

CONTINUED READING IMPROVEMENT

Having been put through the improvement course described in this book, it is our hope that all students will experience some improvement in their reading. The question that now arises is 'Have the students reached their maximum reading potential?' or 'Would they be able to progress in speed and comprehension even further?' Probably no student ever reaches his maximum potential, and certainly not in a ten-week course. But the teacher can only concentrate on improving reading ability by such methods as timed reading drill and comprehension tests for a limited period of time before it begins to get boring. It is probably best not to prolong a reading-improvement course indefinitely; and it is intended that the course described in this book should be part of the whole English course. It is recommended that having completed the course as described in this book the teacher proceed to other aspects of language teaching. There are, however, a few points out of this course that might be kept in mind for future practice.

First of all, the teacher might consider giving another course similar to this one at another time, say a year or more later. Perhaps at some other time, within a year of this course, the teacher might give a few timed reading exercises to remind students that speed is important and that all thought of keeping up reading speed should not be abandoned when a specific reading course is completed. So it is recommended that from time to time a short series of timed reading exercises be given to remind the student of the importance of reading speed.

In describing the *Drill Book*, which has multiple-choice questions emphasizing objective and subjective comprehension, we have stressed an important part of reading comprehension. But reading comprehension has many other aspects. The teacher undoubtedly knows how to teach some of them. He might ask the class to answer simple and complex recall questions (for example—a complex question 'What was the main point of this story? Write one paragraph'). The use of comprehension questions of other kinds than multiple-choice is recommended.

Reading comprehension should of course be taught in a number of subjects. History books or mathematics books might easily be used for reading comprehension practice. Some 'readers' have comprehension questions following the stories. These comprehension exercises provide interesting and useful emphasis on comprehension.

The student should not forget how to skim, and it would be well if the teacher from time to time would give skimming practice. Students might skim magazines, newspapers, or books, and report the results to the class. They need to be reminded that skimming is a valuable and useful tool to be used when time is short and comprehension need not be too high.

In the same way the students can be reminded of the study technique mentioned in this book when homework is set. If before setting homework, or telling the students that there will be an examination in a certain subject, the teacher reviews the SQ3R or some of the other study principles, it may serve as a useful and timely reminder to the student that there are certain ways of studying which are better than others.

Finally, there is nothing that improves reading like reading. If the student reads a lot, he will continue to improve. Easy reading is good for him and hard reading is good for him. Skimming is good, reading for pleasure is good, and studying is good. But too much of one and none of the other is bad.

It is hoped that through this reading course the student has acquired the techniques that will enable him to read more efficiently and with much more pleasure.

SUMMARY AND SUGGESTED LECTURE OUTLINE

1. Vocabulary develops rapidly with use and with each year of education. Educated people know many thousands of words.

2. Vocabulary helps to determine the difficulty of reading material. The difficulty of a book (i.e. the size of its vocabulary) is sometimes stated.

3. The teacher should match the student's reading ability against the difficulty of a book by hearing the student read it aloud. See Table 8 (for 'basic', 'instruction' and 'frustration' levels) and Appendix 1.

4. Teach vocabulary building by (1) word families—roots, prefixes, etc.; and (2) mental underlining.

5. All use of language, both in school and out, helps reading comprehension.

6. Students should have variety in reading both in subject and in difficulty.

7. Encourage students to read more by starting book clubs, talking about books in class, giving time in school for recreational reading, and matching books to the students' interests.

8. Continued reading improvement might be aided by
   different types of comprehension test, such as those with
   'recall' not multiple-choice questions, and
   comprehension practice in different subjects, such as
   mathematics and history.

During the year the teacher might from time to time give speed tests similar to those in the *Drill Book*, skimming exercises, and a review of study techniques.

9. This course is intended to be only one part of reading development, so the teacher should not try to prolong this course until it becomes boring, thereby neglecting other important aspects of English.

APPENDIX 1

JUDGING THE READABILITY
OF BOOKS

Selecting the right reading material for his pupils is one of a teacher's most important jobs. If he gives a student material that is too hard for him, the student will become bored with it and may stop reading, or his comprehension of the material will be poor. Even if he does struggle through it, it will take an excessive amount of time. On the other hand, if the student is given material that is too easy (which is not often the case) he may find it 'babyish' and again become bored and stop reading.

The basic interest in the subject itself is of course an important factor. Given a very high interest, the student may work through very difficult material. But on the average, given only a normal amount of interest in the subject-matter, if the material is too difficult the student will stop reading. And most teachers would agree that it is very important for students to read, and read widely and frequently, if they are to be properly educated.

Hence, this appendix is concerned with a specific method of judging readability. Some teachers may say 'Oh, I can tell from looking at a book how difficult it is'. This may be true in a few instances, but most teachers cannot. Studies have shown that readability formulae, for all their faults, are more reliable than teachers' judgements. Readability formulae tend to be stiff and mechanical and often those who love English prose distrust them. But teachers who love children and wish to see them learn at a maximum rate might well give heed to readability formulae as an important aid to their judgement.

The use of a readability formula is valuable only if the teacher knows the reading ability of the student. Unfortunately, teachers do not always know the reading ability of each student— promotion to the next class is not always a guarantee of reading ability. The teacher should use standardized oral or silent

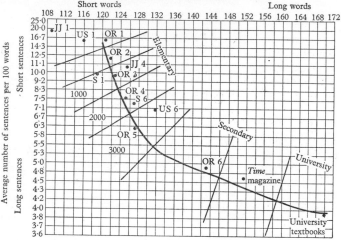

Fig. 31. Graph for estimating readability; see p. 137.

reading tests. If no standardized tests are available there are many reading text-books which will tell the teacher how to make his or her own.

If neither tests nor text-books are available, here is a simple general principle that can be followed. Take any set of graded reading text-books for children and have each child read several paragraphs from several books. The student should be able to pronounce 95 % of the words and after silent reading answer questions on the material with 75 % accuracy or better if the material is to be considered as at 'instructional level'. This means that the book in question can be used in class where help is available. But for reading at home or for pleasure he should pronounce an even higher percentage of the words (99 out of 100) and have a higher comprehension. But, and here is the most important point, if the child cannot pronounce 95 % of the words (at least 19 out of 20) and his comprehension is below 75 %, then the book should not be used even for instruction. Get an easier book.

You can teach reading (and every other subject) much better if you have books at the right level of difficulty: in fact, if you

136

An attempt was made to make this graph and formula simple and universal. By universal we mean that it can be used with whatever series of reading-instruction books the school system is using. We have plotted the Oxford English Readers for Africa ('OR 1', 'OR 2', etc.) simply to illustrate how the formula might be used. A few other reference points are also given on the graph for well-known British and American readers. 'JJ 1' and 'JJ 4' stand for the British *Janet and John* primary-school readers (by Mabel O'Donnell and Rona Monroe; James Nisbet and Co., 1949). 'S 1' and 'S 6' stand for the Schonell *Wide Range Readers* often used in British schools after completion of the *Janet and John* series. Schonell states that his first book (S 1) represents a reading age of 7–7½ years while his sixth book (S 6) represents a reading age of 10+ to 11+. 'US 1' and 'US 6' are representative of United States reading books, the sample being taken from the Gates MacMillan readers for the first and sixth grades which are usually used by children of ages 6½ and 12.

Since pupils in Africa and many other countries usually begin to read in English several years later because it is their second language, this study indicates that perhaps they could begin with books that use an easier vocabulary load. Books more nearly approaching those used by American or British beginning readers might give foreign students more initial success and interest in reading English.

It is interesting that most books will fall in the area of the chart near the curve and its cross lines. Very few writers use long words and short sentences or vice versa. It is also interesting that in the 'Elementary section' most of the discrimination of difficulty is by sentence length, while in the higher levels vocabulary plays an increasingly more important part. (Writers of simplified material must not use this formula for more than a cross-check; they should work from vocabulary lists.)

can get a student reading, by giving him easy interesting materials, and if you simply keep him reading, gradually increasing the difficulty of the material, you will have gone a long way towards having a very good reading programme. Do not worry about the material being too easy, especially where students have difficulty with reading; they will gradually seek more difficult material. Too many teachers start with difficult material and then wonder why students hate to read and avoid it at every opportunity.

At Makerere University College Institute of Education, the Dean, Mr John Bright, asked me to work on the problem of developing a simple readability formula for use in African schools. The first procedure was to study the best-known readability formulae used in the United States, try them out and see what went into them. Some were discarded because they were too complicated or needed special devices, tables or vocabularies. I decided that fairly reliable results could be obtained by using just two criteria: vocabulary load and grammatical complexity.

There are two main ways of determining vocabulary load. The first is by using a set vocabulary, of say 3000 common words, and then counting all words not in this list. The second is to count the number of syllables in a hundred words. I chose the syllable-counting method because it was easier and needed less training and equipment.

There are several ways of determining grammatical complexity, such as counting prepositional phrases, etc., but fortunately (as was found in some earlier work of Mr Peter Wingard at Makerere) they all seemed to correlate with sentence length. So I chose sentence length as the simplest measure of grammatical complexity.

The formula presented in Fig. 31 I call a readability 'estimate' because it is probably not as accurate as the best formulae (in my opinion the Spache for lower forms and the Dale Chall for upper forms and adult classes—these formulae can be found reprinted in *Research in the 3 R's*, edited by Hunicutt and Iverson, Harper, New York, 1959). On the other hand my formula does not require use of long vocabularies or mathematical computations. It has a further advantage in that by using a chart as I have done, the teacher can pencil in his own criteria. For example, I have given the approximate position of the Oxford English Readers for Africa. Teachers who know that one of their students can read at say the Oxford Reader Level 3 can then select other books at or below that level for that student to read. If, however, the teacher uses any other series of readers he can simply work out the formula for each book in the series and plot it on the graph, thereby creating his own readability standard.

DIRECTIONS FOR USING THE FORMULA

(1) Select three 100 word passages from near the beginning, middle, and end of the book.

(2) Count the total number of sentences in each 100 word passage (estimating to the nearest tenth of a sentence). Average these three numbers (add together and divide by three).

(3) Count the total number of syllables in each 100 word sample. There is a syllable for each vowel sound; for example: *cat* (1), *blackbird* (2), *continental* (4). Do not be deceived by word size, for example: *polio* (3), *through* (1). Endings such as *-y*, *-el*, or *-le* usually make a syllable, for example: *ready* (2), *bottle* (2). Average the total number of syllables for the three samples.

(4) Plot on the graph the average number of sentences per hundred words. If it falls near Oxford Reader 5 for example, you can say that the book is of about the same difficulty as Oxford Reader 5.

	Sentences per 100 words	Syllables per 100 words
100 word sample page 5	9·1	122
100 word sample page 89	8·5	140
100 word sample page 160	7·0	129
Divide total by 3	3 ⟌24·6	3 ⟌391
Average	8·2	130

Plotting these averages on the graph we see that they fall near the 'OR 4'; thus this book is about as hard to read as the fourth Oxford Reader.

Table 13. An example of the formula in use.

A further estimate of difficulty level is given on the graph by the words 'Elementary', 'Secondary', and 'University', which of course refer to levels of schooling. Some publishers, particularly those who publish 'adapted' or abridged books useful for normal schoolchildren, retarded learners, and foreign students, grade the difficulty of their books by stating that 'this book uses a 2000 word vocabulary except for a few subject-matter words', etc. Thus the '1000, 2000, 3000' notation on the chart is an attempt to correlate this system of grading. Unfortunately, publishers and authors of these 'adapted' books do not always use the same 1000 word vocabulary; they do not all stick to it as closely as they might; and, worse still, some authors of simplified material, while paying attention to vocabulary, do not pay attention to the sentence structure.

CONCLUSION

This formula can be used as an aid in determining the difficulty of reading material. While it is objective and mechanical it is sometimes more accurate than subjective evaluation. In any event it is not intended to replace the judgement of an experienced teacher but rather to act as a valuable supplement. The purpose is to help teachers to match the difficulty level of reading material with the reading ability of the student. Other factors which contribute towards making material easier to read are large clear type, familiarity with the subject matter, and helpful illustrations; but these factors should not override consideration of the more basic factors of vocabulary difficulty and sentence structure.

Every school library should have at least one shelf of books that have been graded according to difficulty. The level of difficulty (for example 'OR 5') should be marked on every book graded, inside the back cover or on the binding. Often the teacher can train several of his older students to work the formula on new library books as they arrive. The formula might also help teachers and administrators in selecting text-books.

APPENDIX 2

A MEMORY TRICK

The following is (1) an interesting parlour trick with which the student can interest and amuse his friends, (2) a serious experiment in psychology which clearly demonstrates the power of associative learning, and (3) a useful skill that can sometimes help the student to remember a long and not necessarily related list of facts (useful in passing some examinations and in going to the grocery shop).

First let us give an example of how the parlour trick might be done in school. The student asks his friends to call out slowly a list of objects—any objects. The friends call out 'clock-chair-hammer', etc. Often a friend will write them down on the blackboard so that the others will not forget them: '1, clock; 2, chair; 3, hammer'. The student does not look at the blackboard. After twenty objects, or however many the students decide, he calls a halt and immediately announces that he has memorized all the objects and that he can call them out in any order—forwards, backwards, every other way—in fact he can tell his friends the number of any object (without looking at the board). The friends say that they do not believe him; one of them asks 'What is number 3'? The student immediately replies, 'Hammer'. Then after a few such questions he proves his complete mastery by calling off the whole list either forwards or backwards.

Now almost anyone can do this trick, once he knows how. The secret lies in first memorizing a set of 'key objects'. You must first take a little time to memorize (make mental associations between) a 'key object' and the number. For example, the key object for number one is 'sun' and the key object for number two is 'shoe', etc. (see the list on the following page). You must first learn the association between the key object and the number so well that whenever you say 'one' to yourself you visualize 'sun'. You should easily be able to learn the first ten key objects and their numbers in a short learning session on the first day, ten more the next day, and so on. After you have learned the key objects well you are ready to do the trick. When the first friend calls out the word 'clock' as the first thing for you to memorize, you must mentally picture a 'clock' next to a 'sun' which is your object for number 1. After you have made a clear mental picture of a clock next to a sun you then allow the next friend to call out a second thing to be memorized, such as 'chair'; you then mentally picture a chair with your key object, a shoe, sitting on it. You control the rate at which your friends can call out names of objects; at first you will go rather slowly but after you have done the trick a few times you can go more rapidly.

Key objects

1	Sun	11	Elephant
2	Shoe	12	Twig
3	Tree	13	Throne
4	Door	14	Fort
5	Hive	15	Fire
6	Sticks	16	Silver coin
7	Heaven (an angel)	17	Sea
8	Gate	18	Apron
9	Sign	19	Knife
10	Pen	20	Baby

There are several important learning principles involved in this trick which also apply to other learning. One is the 'mental visualization'—it is a powerful factor in memory, and can be developed with relatively little practice. Another important factor is self-confidence on the part of the student; if he says beforehand 'I can't do it' he probably won't be able to. Self-confidence is also important during the trick, for you must concentrate only on the object to be remembered, you cannot worry about 'Did I learn the first three things?' Exaggeration of mental pictures, making them large, brightly coloured, or even purposefully distorted, will often aid memory.

This type of memorizing is not a new discovery. It was well known by the ancient people of both Greece and India.

The key objects listed above have been chosen to take advantage of another learning principle; that of rhyming. The first ten objects all have an end-rhyme with the name of the number.

The second ten objects all begin with the same sound as the name of the number, except for 20, where a rough rhyme is used to avoid confusion with 12. If the student wishes to extend the list of objects to 50 or 100, or change any of the suggested list below, he can choose any 'key objects' that he wishes. The important thing is that they be easily visualized and never change.